THE FALL of the AMERICAN UNIVERSITY

ADAM ULAM

THE FALL of the AMERICAN UNIVERSITY

THE LIBRARY PRESS
New York
1972

Library of Congress Catalog Card Number:
77-39004

International Standard Book Number:
0-912050-20-9

Printed in the United States of America

Contents

PREFACE

THERE ARE MANY who believe that the crisis of the American university is over. Students have stopped rioting, universities have become innovative and responsive to community needs; all is well again. In fact, the plight of American higher education is worse than it was three or four years ago, though certainly not as spectacular. Riots have, by and large, disappeared, but the politicization and bureaucratization of the American university have grown apace, with the corresponding shrinking of the university's proper function, that of teaching and research.

This book seeks to discern reasons for this unfortunate development which, if unchecked, would lead not only to an educational but to a national calamity: the erosion of the American university as a civilized and civilizing force. To anticipate my argument, these reasons antedate the folly of Vietnam, have little to do with the students' real or alleged grievances and aspirations, and lie in a number of basic misconceptions about what the university can or ought to be. Over the last twenty years there has grown a belief, as erroneous as it is basically incompatible with democracy, that the university can and ought to instruct society on how to conduct its affairs; that those who instruct and administer it possess, quite apart from their professional qualifications, some special wisdom unavailable to the ordinary citizen and which entitles them, in fact puts them under a special obligation, to prescribe cures for social ills, solutions for foreign policy dilemmas, and the like. This claim has had the natural but paradoxical consequence that while trying, and in most cases failing, to do what it should *not* do, the university has increasingly surrendered its authority to do what it *should* do: to run its own affairs with minimum interference by governmental authorities at all levels, pressure groups of all kinds, and by the trends and fashions of the moment.

The educational process is, or at least should be, different from the political one. It is a virtue of democracy that it is responsive to pressures and passions of the moment, that only its basic principles remain free from the processes of bargaining and compromise. But not so with education; it must adhere to basic rules which remain free from the excitements of a season, and which find their source in the rational argument alone. We have seen in the past and in other societies what has happened to schools which have allowed extraneous considerations, no matter how tempting in their alleged solicitude for the general welfare, to affect their educational policies and processes. They have allowed themselves to become seats of obscurantism, of political and philosophical partisanship rather than of learning, sources of national weakness and cultural and scientific backwardness rather than of strength.

And so the current prodigious effort and expense which American society is investing in higher education may still lead to the same and unfortunate results unless the American university is restored to its proper functions.

Adam B. Ulam

Cambridge, Mass.
January 1972

1
Old and New Days

ONE cannot, it seems, get hold of the problem. Is there something wrong with the University? Well, we are told, it is really the problem of the young. What, then, ails the young? In answer we are admonished to take a look at American society. But even here there is no exit from the maze for, as is often repeated, this is a world-wide problem. There are no easy answers. It would be surprising if this sacramental phrase in regard to so many of our current dilemmas and anxieties were not to recur in the report of the Presidential Commission on unrest on the campuses, along with other by now venerable clichés about the generation gap, alienation, the need for restructuring, etc. We all agree that the wretched war has had something to do with our current troubles. But how much? Certainly student unrest exists in countries which do not have a war to cope with, which have disclaimed ambitious overseas roles and burdens: France, Germany, Japan. Is there some fatal flaw in the nature of modern industrial society which generates this unhappiness and its turbulent expressions? "What is the answer?" asked Gertrude

Stein on her deathbed; and after a pause, "what is the question?" Here, then, we begin.

What has happened to the American university? Perhaps, by looking at this institution (which has become crucial in the last twenty-five years) in American life, we shall find at least a partial clue to our current discontents. And perhaps it is better to eschew statistics and elaborate comparisons and to rely on one's own impressions of the changing academic scene in the course of one generation.

In 1945 when I entered the graduate school at Harvard, the university, like the rest of American society, was rather pleased with itself and rather in a non-reflective mood. A popular war was drawing to a victorious end. Apprehensions about the forthcoming peace were felt by a few, but to most the overwhelming reality was the overwhelming character of the victory, as it then seemed, and the consciousness of the stupendous power and vitality of American society, which the war demonstrated after the calamity of the Depression and the gray years which followed it. The first postwar years brought a pleasant surprise and relief: the gloomy forebodings of a recession were laid to rest. Before World War II the university world, one felt, had resigned itself to the conditions of penury, stagnation, and private institutions to a gradual economic decline. Now, to the stupefaction of most economists and administrators, universities and colleges were to experience, like the country at large, a period of fantastic growth and prosperity, and no one as yet could foretell how dangerous this prosperity, and how harmful some aspects of this growth, were to prove to both society and its schools.

The disturbing developments on the international scene served only to enhance the university's and the academic community's standing and functions. Science had become the country's first line of defense. Not far behind physicists and chemists came economists and other social scientists soon needed for the planning and administration of vast schemes of economic aid abroad. In general, the great expansion by this country of its commitments and obligations throughout the world led to the continued connection between the universities and the government. This connection was then viewed neither as elevating the level of the Administration to some new heights as was to be the impression in the early 1960s, nor as sinister complicity of the academy with the military-industrial complex as it was to become fashionable in some circles to believe in the late '60s. It was felt to be, and to some extent was, a natural consequence of the government requiring all of a sudden a great number of experts in all sorts of fields which modern times and America's new role required over and beyond the traditional civil servant. In the period I refer to (the late 1940s and early '50s) the professor in government was viewed not as a messenger from beyond the pedestrian circle of politicians and bureaucrats summoned to formulate strategies in international conflicts, lay down the law to the generals, or to devise more breathtaking plans of domestic reform, the role which sometimes, and often unfortunately, he was to assume later on; he was an expert and consultant in the strict sense of the term, and as such "on tap rather than on top" as somebody very properly described the proper place of the expert in a democratic society.

The new importance and excitement of the learned profession was reflected, of course, within the colleges and universities. Yet apart from the glamor and awe aroused by those who helped devise such shattering advances in nuclear technology, radar, etc., the dominant figure on the campus was still the scholar-teacher rather than the constant voyager to Washington, the "in-and-outer" as the phrase was to have it some fifteen years later, and the professional administrator and/or expert on what ails our youth, society, and the world. This type, soon to move through the foundations, college presidencies, higher echelons of the federal bureaucracy, was already visible, and acquiring the sobriquet of *philanthropoid,* but he was not as frequent and disturbing a phenomenon as now.

The university, in brief, was basking in its new and pleasing importance and prosperity, but it did not seek nor was it expected by the students or the public to save the world, destroy peacefully or otherwise the Establishment, solve psychological and religious problems of its members, enthrone democracy and social justice throughout the land. It was expected to be itself: a place of learning and hence enjoyment. The new role, the influx of veterans, eager to enjoy themselves but also to get through their studies and to start upon a career, imparted to the American college of the time an additional feeling of vitality and purpose. The university of those days appears in retrospect different from both the college before 1939, then an enclave of privilege if not indeed largely country club or finishing school in its spirit, and from the institution in the 1960s beset not only by student turbulence and politicization, but even more by the underlying doubts as to its purpose and usefulness to society. The representative student of those days seemed, to me at least, to have been endowed with certain sober grace and gaiety and (perhaps because of that) maturity distinct at once from the frivolity of the Joe College type of the prewar years, and that humorless earnestness and hence a craving for excitement which beset a sizeable element of the young today (though not as many as we would be led to believe by the magazines and some bureaucrats and educators). The freshly acquired status of the academic profession led to its growing prestige in the community at large, popularity and, most important, self-confidence. Few would have foreseen how, as in recent years, that outlook would give way to exaggerated claims by some of its members as well as to a widespread loss of morale, and bitterness against the society which having given the university so much and held out the prospects of more has made it the main battleground of its anxieties and disappointments.

One cannot feel nostalgic about the American university between 1945-1955 any more than one feels about American society of that period. There were too many injustices and defects crying for remedies. One felt that the enormous strength and wealth of the country was not being used either at home or abroad with the intelligence nearly commensurate with its resources and opportunities. But one does and ought to feel nostalgic about the *direction* the university as well as the country at large was taking in those years. One sensed in both a certain pragmatism and briskness in dealing with outstanding problems which were appropriate to a free society. The miasmas, doubts, and dogmatic views spawned by the Depression appeared to have been left behind. Panic and irrationality would surge forth occasionally, as during the Korean conflict and as seen in its progeny McCarthyism. But the common sense of a democracy would soon, though not as soon as it should have, subdue them. One had the feeling, which currently appears to have been an illusion, of a society gradually overcoming the legacy of neurotic puritanism as well as of vulgar materialism and simplistic democracy. Simple-minded nationalism, evident in that morbid fear of "un-American" activities and sentiments, appeared to be yielding to greater sophistication and awareness and appreciation of the outside world. Disrespect for and impatience with learning promised to be replaced by a balanced view of the role and place of the intellectual. Concrete remedies were being proposed and sometimes enacted for real social evils. Colleges and universities, because they were not trying self-consciously to change society, were in fact contributing a great deal to social change as well as to the spread of knowledge. Of course, as we shall see, things were not going *quite* so well. There were some disturbing developments which would mature into today's horror.

Today many will decry even such modest and qualified nostalgia and will argue, or rather, in the current fashion, shout that the university as well as the whole country fifteen and twenty years ago was not facing the real problems, was complacent, etc. But whatever the progress and alleged greater frankness in facing them today, the disturbing thing is the spirit in which they are now approached. Everything touching on major areas of social unhappiness appears enveloped in a moralistic haze. The university as well as the country is not so much asked to tackle actual problems, such as student participation in the case of one, poverty in the case of the other, but to don a hairshirt, to acknowledge its guilt, to go on trying to change and reform, but always with the consciousness that it can never *fully* atone for sins of the past and present. It is not as men impatient for relief and improvement but it is with a masochistic feeling of fulfillment that we are to acknowledge the presence of pollution, racial violence, etc. Suddenly we seem to be thrust into the Dark Ages, but at least then there were real hairshirts, acts of penance and contrition available to free the individual from the unbearable sense of guilt, and to enable him to deal with the business of life. Now we are supposed to restructure everything: domestic priorities, foreign policy, our schools, but all along chanting "we are guilty, we've been guilty."

BUT, BACK TO the university. In comparison with the institution of our day, it was in 1945—just as the America of that day appears contrasted with this country today—backward, *i.e.,* much poorer, more primitive. Why, there were still a lot of farmers, *only* twenty-five million or so private automobiles, there were still passenger trains. The revolution of rising expectations was just beginning, that of catastrophic apprehension which we are now undergoing not yet in sight. And so with the university: the catalogue of courses offered under the Faculty of Arts and Sciences was less than half as thick as it is today. University buildings were old, often in bad condition. Since the Depression and the completion of the Harvard Houses, the only new building added was, I believe, the Littauer Center housing the School of Public Administration. Some extremely primitive living quarters were constructed to house the influx of veterans. In a few years the veterans were gone, the huts which housed them and their families were dismantled and replaced by the huge graduate dormitory complex. The period of growth was on.

Faculty recruitment and promotion reflected the penury and economic vicissitudes of the era which was just ending. The schedule of appointments insured that barring new endowment funds, every department or school could just replenish its existing staff. Some unfortunate experiences before the war led to careful provisions that the number of non-permanent positions should not be too large in relation to prospective openings among the senior and permanent faculty. Promotions had been slow, some people of great distinction, and even reputation, not reaching the grade of full professor before their late forties and even fifties. There was, in brief, an atmosphere of penury and even of certain shabbiness about this the richest private university in the country, and one may draw certain general conclusions about the state of American higher education on the morrow of the Second World War. Today in this respect at Harvard as well as elsewhere, we live in an era of incongruity: new buildings are springing up, faculties are rapidly expanding, yet those more numerous professors working in their more comfortable offices, lecturing in more elegant lecture rooms are subject to strains unimaginable in the late 1940s, and their real income can barely if at all keep up with the new inflationary pressures. The era of professorial affluence which beckoned so enticingly a decade or so ago appears, alas, to have been as a mirage. Along with society at large the universities have been first beneficiaries, then victims of growth.

The poorer shabbier university of a generation ago was still an institution of learning. On this count, again, there is no room for unreserved nostalgia. It was a pleasant myth, but a myth nevertheless, that even a leading university like Harvard had a uniformly excellent faculty, that there were no incompetent people on the staff, that extraneous considerations did not enter into any appointments. Today the general level of what might be called technical competence is undoubtedly much higher in practically every institution of higher learning. Insofar as such an institution is at all respectable, there is much less of a gap between it and Chicago, Berkeley, or Harvard than was the case. And yet . . .

In those days of yore it was obvious and rather encouraging that you did not have this nervous anxiety on the part of the university administration and trustees that *every* part of the structure was equally important, that every existing or fashionable discipline should be supported or endowed with an eye to what *X* university is doing in this field, and we are perhaps, God forbid, falling behind. It was, I feel, far from tragic that the Harvard School of Education at the time had few teachers, students or funds. It was far from clear to me then, as it is now, why teaching at the intermediate and elementary levels should require a highly specialized curriculum and why it could not be undertaken by any so inclined college graduate after a period of supervised training and apprenticeship. Coming from the Continent, it struck me odd then (and it does now) that there should be such a thing as a non-denominational school of divinity within what was frankly a secular university. Within the then miniscule faculty of the said school there were great scholars; but they could be contained in departments of history and philosophy, without bearing this rather constraining and puzzling professional obligation to some non-denominational diety. The "benign neglect" in which the two schools had been left for some time could be seen as a wise form of university restructuring: an obsolete relic of the past as well as the product of an unfortunate educational fashion were being left to expire peacefully and unsensationally. Anyway, there were plenty of schools of theology and education in the country, to which people so inclined could repair. Harvard did not, after all, have a school of agriculture or of home economics. But there came an era of prosperity and the beginnings of one of anxiety. What was Harvard doing for the nation's schools? And is not theology, even if non-denominational, an antidote to subversion, and a flourishing divinity school a crushing answer to those who believe that higher education subverts the faith in God and country? (This was during the earlier part of McCarthy's era.) Funds were solicited, chairs were endowed, the two schools were rescued from the brink of extinction. How the professed aims of this resurrection have been served I shall discreetly refrain from discussing, at least for now.

Everybody has his own idea of what the proper province of instruction and research is. But the notion which was to blossom during the prosperous and unapprehensive years of the 1950s that *everything* important and desirable in the fields of learning, arts, etc. should be covered by *every* major university must be now seen as a mistake. Many of those things can best be instructed and developed outside a formal academic structure. Creative arts, for instance, may flourish in a university community, but are better off without the necessarily confining institutional ties, departments, etc. A Tolstoy formed by a college course in creative writing is as unimaginable as is an Einstein learning mathematics all by himself. Of course, instructions in creative writing, musical composition, etc. are all to the good, but somehow the highest artistic skills and expressions are not likely to flourish in a classroom atmosphere. Yet even here the universities advanced boldly: Harvard now has a Department of Visual Arts. Why should one so ungraciously begrudge to some students the opportunity to do sculpture, photography, etc. as part of their college training? Well, this small point leads to a larger one: the university, even the richest, the best equipped one, etc., simply cannot attend to all the needs of young men and women, ought not pretend that all their major dimensions of development can receive nourishment and impetus within its shelter. One has confronted in recent years increasing complaint by undergraduates that they do not find in their education anything "creative." But the university's main and honorable function is to transmit knowledge. An unusual teacher may strike off a spark in an unusual student which will lead the latter to be a creative scientist, writer or artist. But as such an academic institution cannot be *expected* to fulfill artistic needs of a few, just as it cannot fulfill religious cravings of many. This is, then, one aspect of arousing excessive expectations, of the university claiming to be not just one institution of many fulfilling an extremely important but of necessity limited function, but the master institution of modern society not only teaching and advancing knowledge, but being the seat of virtue and social wisdom, the vehicle for political reform, providing something no social institution by itself or even all of them together can give: a feeling of happiness and fulfillment to all its members. No school can be life, it can offer, at most, preparation for life.

Apart from this simple point, but one of which we have unaccountably lost sight, there were obvious economic reasons why the striving to bring everything important and desirable under the university's roof was bound to have deleterious effects. A distinguished school cannot consciously tolerate academic slums, so to speak, cannot admit that Department *X* is scandalously weak or far below the level of other branches of instruction. And there were such, even at Harvard. But the business of keeping up with the academic Joneses in everything is obviously unreasonable and wasteful. At least in a country as vast and with so many institutions of higher learning as the United States. There should be (and, to some extent, there has been) a division of labor between the leading universities in this country: one would be particularly strong in physical sciences, another in history, biology, etc. But in recent and prosperous years, an unfortunate type of institutional chauvinism was allowed to sweep the country. It was encouraged by those educational surveys gravely assigning standings and points to universities as if they were baseball teams arousing institutional neuroses amongst the administrators: "Good God, we are fifth in sociology and last in Egyptology!" This competition was joined to a much more harmful one: the rage to build and expand physical facilities. It is pleasant to have spacious and elegant dormitories, classrooms, and office buildings. What might be called the Pharaonic complex of the college administrators has always been very strong, and of course the benefactors would always want to be immortalized in brick and stone.

On these counts Harvard then offered an example of admirable self-restraint. Its relatively well-paid professors sat in rather shabby offices. Its students did not feel unduly handicapped by living in overcrowded undergraduate houses and the graduate dormitories, some of which with a few alterations could have been readily transformed into model penitentiaries. One does not want to extol discomfort, and may doubt the wisdom of the philosophy of the English public school with its cold showers and corresponding level of living conditions for the pupils. All one pleads for is a sense of proportion. There is now many a spacious and expensive office building, bringing "under one roof" (as its rationale always runs) people in various disciplines who previously were dispersed throughout many buildings (why do they *have* to be under one roof?). Yet the salaries are lagging, scholarship funds are inadequate, and Harvard's great asset and glory, its library, is experiencing financial troubles.

During the first postwar years, Harvard, fairly uniquely among similar institutions, had the fortitude to resist the temptation to imbibe largely of the federal funds. This heroic restraint and self-denial was, alas, not to continue for very long. There began a small trickle, before long a veritable flood. Until the middle 1950s there could be some smugness over the fact that a sudden end of the Cold War, and/or the enthronement in power in Washington of partisans of retrenchment and economy (of the brand of the late Senator Taft) would have meant a veritable castastrophe to places like M.I.T., much if not most of whose budget now relied on government funds and contracts, but that Harvard, though not unhurt, would go on. But then there was to be no resisting of an overwhelming trend. Of course the pressure was really irresistible as far as science facilities were concerned: no private institution could afford cyclotrons, etc. In fields like medicine and public health, government support is both necessary and proper. But the taxpayers' money was also massively applied to projects, inquiries, and researches in the social sciences. Various techniques and analyses, which were to be used by our policy-makers in Southeast Asia and elsewhere, were developed in academic surroundings, some here in Cambridge, and this was to cause the furor during the last few years. But some of the strongest assailants of the university's complicity in the schemes of the military-industrial complex had, it was to turn out, their own researches and studies demonstrating the iniquity of American capitalism-imperialism financed by the same source. The ROTC was chased out of the Harvard campus, just as it was out of many others, by the aroused and indignant faculty and students. Some of the most vocal and instrumental in this expulsion were on government scholarships, their allies and mentors on the faculty, recipients of government grants.

THE PROBLEM is a hard one, the need for government assistance in certain fields obvious and unavoidable. Yet common sense, again, would have urged greater restraint. A university is not an independent enclave in society, its students and personnel not bound by the laws and obligations which apply to the common herd, as some believe it ought to be and is. But, within this framework, independence of the government, whether the relevant agency is the Defense or the Health, Education, and Welfare Department, is a very precious thing. It has accounted, in the past, for the great and beneficial difference in character between the British and American universities and the continental ones, the former being much freer of political interference, of student unrest. It was fatuous to expect that the private schools could take a lot of money from the state and yet remain free of pressures and entanglements with the government. It is unreasonable and unjust to expect that the taxpayer or Congress can be expected to spend vast sums and yet remain indifferent as to how it is being used. What was most disturbing was, as is always the case in such things, the fuzzing of the issue. If beyond a certain point an institution becomes dependent on support of the state, then it is hard to see how it still can claim complete immunity from criticism and direction from the authority which supports it. A high degree of financial dependence by a private institution on the government is in itself neither evil nor beneficial; it is simply destructive of that concept of education which has been traditional in this country, and if this tradition can no longer be maintained, then it should be changed consciously and openly.

How was the university governed? Here indeed in the 1940s and '50s one found huge differences. Tolstoy begins *Anna*

Karenina with the famous observation that every happy family is happy in the same way, every unhappy one in its unique manner. One may say the reverse about institutions of higher learning, perhaps institutions in general. Every unhappy university, *i.e.*, practically every university in recent years, has been unhappy in the same way: one of the symptoms of this unhappiness being excessive attention, prominence and dispute as to how this institution is governed. In those far distant days, in fact until three or four years ago, this problem loomed important mostly in small schools. A friend of mine upon his "liberation," *i.e.*, on leaving a small school, announced that he was going to write a study of the small American college as a model of totalitarian community. An exaggeration, to be sure, yet many such a school practiced its own brand of the cult of personality, outwardly reminding one of that adopted by the late Joseph Stalin. Its landscape was dominated by the president, this potentate's exhortations, statements, jokes, crowding the pages of its alumni magazine, featured upon each ceremony and celebration, he being depicted in countless poses of command, beamed at by the alumni, looked at with awe by the students, feared by his faculty. Lo and behold! recently he has become a figure of tragedy, depicted as smiling but this time nervously and pleadingly, his audience wrathful and unappeased. In the large state universities the president was not a benevolent despot: there were trustees and regents appointed by the legislature. The academic leader was, rather, a mediator and, if successful, a magician capable of unlocking the coffers of the taxpayers, capable of soothing their apprehensions about the scandalous political views of Professor X who mentioned Karl Marx in his course or talked about free love.

In relatively few fortunate schools, Harvard being one, the personality and powers of the president, trustees, etc. were of little or no interest to the students and faculty. I doubt whether as much as one student out of a hundred, one teacher out of ten, did in the year of grace 1946 spend any time at all thinking about the intricate structure of the university government at Harvard, or thought it of any importance to the business at hand or his own happiness. The government, *i.e.,* the president had the so-called governing boards, came into prominence once a year during the commencement when they performed the appropriate ritual. There was more awareness of and contact with those dignitaries among the alumni: they were of obvious importance in fund-raising and for public relations. But to the average member of the college community the president was a bit like the Mikado during the Shogunate in Japan: the ceremonial head and representative of the institution as a whole yet distant from its problems and cares. It was felt proper that the incumbent was a distinguished scientist and a person of national prominence, and yet this was of no overwhelming importance. This lack of interest was a healthy phenomenon for it indicated—a mark of a healthy institution—that people were interested in their own jobs and left other people to do theirs. In the academic community at large there was to be but little surprise and opposition when soon a great war hero was elevated to the presidency of a great university (Eisenhower at Columbia), and a lesser one to that of a smaller school (Governor Stassen at Pennsylvania). The president, it was felt, could affect but little the essentials of the functioning of an institution of learning, he could impart some dignity to its leadership, deliver appropriate speeches upon appropriate occasions and loosen the strings of the alumni's purses. But how could he change anything in the teaching of physics or constitutional history? And *that* was important. It would have been felt inappropriate and probably would have been resisted had Eisenhower been proposed as history professor and Governor Stassen assigned to do regular teaching of political science:

education does not consist in students gaping at a prominent or even a great man and listening to well meant clichés or recollections. It implied no disrespect for military or political achievement, simply a recognition that they had their own sphere, just as learning and teaching theirs. Such opinions may be stigmatized as parochial and snobbish, yet have we been better off since professors have become military and political strategists, and politicians educational statesmen?

There is no denying, of course, that American education owed a great deal to a handful of men who around the turn of the century took their rather primitive and backward (as compared with Europe's best) schools and turned them into real universities which soon equalled and then surpassed their British and German models. But in 1945 one could think and hope that once set in the right direction the leading schools, at least, could go on their momentum and that their example would spread. The president and trustees would remain as the court of last resort but, barring some flagrant abuse, leave the educational and instructional role to the faculty. The latter, in turn, would delegate to its administratively-minded members the task of keeping in touch with the students' needs and opinions and laying down regulations accordingly. Such a sensible division of labor would save everybody's time and would assure a smooth functioning of the whole. There was obviously no sense in the faculty as a body concerning itself at what times young men should be allowed to entertain young ladies in their college rooms (this sounds very antediluvian). Clearly neither the students nor the Corporation (the governing body) was competent to adjudge who should be appointed to a vacancy in mathematics or archaeology, so it was left to other mathematicians and archaeologists. And nobody *then* questioned the fact that the bankers and businessmen of the Corporation were competent to invest the university's funds and deal with problems of its *physical* growth without intruding upon the time and unconcern of the faculty and students. There were problems which could not be disposed of so neatly and which required interaction of several bodies and constituencies: where new funds should be allocated, what new fields of learning required recognition and support, salaries, etc. But generally this principle applied: the university was so organized to enable everybody to do his job, to do what he knew and liked best. The slogans of student or faculty power would have aroused not so much opposition as incomprehension. How is one deprived of power if one is spared the task of doing something one is unqualified to do and does not want to be bothered with anyway?

Wasn't the whole structure hideously undemocratic? Well, we shall consider later the whole problem and how terms like democratic and undemocratic can be meaningfully applied to education. But to anticipate some of the conclusions, can or must every institution in a democracy be democratic? Is public transportation undemocratic because people must get on and off the bus at scheduled stops and even a unanimous vote of the passengers will not make the driver alter the course? Were not the students oppressed by being subject to those arbitrary decisions laid down by several oligarchies: the corporation, deans, the faculty? To most of them this question as well as any insinuation that college rules and regulations deprived them of that "control over their lives" would have appeared highly comical.

This pattern obviously had to change and, in retrospect, it is clear that some techniques for enabling the students and faculty to participate or be consulted should have been developed when the first warnings of the forthcoming troubles appeared ten years ago or so. But here again there is no question that the general principle of the old division of functions was sensible and should have been maintained as far as possible. Today, of course, universal participation is the rage. Wily administrators believe that involving students in "decision-making," *i.e.,* putting them on committees, is a clever way of appeasing them, encouraging moderates *vs.* the extremists, etc. The faculty is supposed to look over the trustees' shoulders as to what *they* are doing, how the university's portfolio of investments is being administered, etc. The trustees, in turn, are supposed to keep in touch with the students' and the faculty's feelings; the administration, in the new lingo, is to be "sensitive" and "responsive," which one must assume means that it should be ready to meet some demands even before they are formulated. Thus the circular flow of concern, or if one prefers, busybodyness.

A student of totalitarian society knows that one of its most noxious features is slavery through forced participation; the extolling of snooping and minding of other people's business is proclaimed as the highest form of altruism. The Soviet and Chinese citizen is constantly dragged to meetings, constantly exhorted, urged to look to his left and right at what his fellow worker, superior and subordinate are doing, expected to report on it, as well as on his own activities and thoughts. The system—*the* leader— is all wise and beneficent, but one's neighbor, supervisor, or fellow worker is always a potential villain or shirker. Thank God we are not there yet as far as the university and American society as a whole are concerned; but there is a disturbing degree of acceptance of the principle that everything is everybody's business. Freedom to mind one's own business is one of the most precious of democratic freedoms; if we lose it, if more and more people are brainwashed to believe that there is something selfish and undemocratic in doing just what one is supposed and qualified to do rather than in worrying what other people are doing, we will undermine much of what is liberal and agreeable in our society.

Within the American university one can observe now what might be called growing participation fatigue. In most cases the great majority of people, students and teachers alike, follow their own interests and jobs. And yet every year in the last half-decade it has become harder to do just that. It is not only that incidents of violence and turbulence have intruded upon previously placid surroundings. Quite apart from them, pressures inimical to work, study and reflection have mounted and exacted an increasing toll. The faculty meeting used to be an infrequent, decorous and unimportant affair. Now they have grown inordinately, in number and length. Even prior to the recent troubles, administrative duties, paperwork and committee meetings have intruded upon the professor's proper work and that leisure which is essential to intellectual work. Now it has become a veritable flood which threatens to engulf us all.

It might be and will be objected that such sentiments betray gross insensitivity. Here, if you please, is a great crisis tearing this nation apart, a whole generation in anguish—and all some of you academic people worry about is the leisure to do your precious monographs, articles, to go on with your teaching so often irrelevant to the cares and needs of today's youth. But here, again, it is honest and best to face the issue directly. No one has proposed shutting down the universities until the whole question of the proper function of higher education and the proper way of administering them is decided. If so, one ought to assume that the traditional function of the university is the proper one, and perhaps especially in times of crisis. Out of the present turmoil there might come, though this is extremely doubtful, a highly ingenious (and acceptable to everybody) system of governing the university, a virtuous, socially relevant and profitable way of investing its funds, an equitable manner of dealing with each group of students' demands and aspirations. But what good would it do if this "restructured" university would produce agitated rather than educated young men, if its faculty, properly "concerned," attuned to socially relevant subjects and engaged in that famous dialogue would be incapable of, would have neither time nor energy to propagate learning? Such prospects may appear, and hopefully are, too bleak. But we have the lesson of those countries, some with great cultural and academic traditions, where the university has become a battleground not so much of politics but of surging irrational emotion. Have learning, social justice, or democracy been the beneficiaries of the chronic unrest in the Latin American, Indian, or Japanese universities?

THE GOVERNANCE OF THE UNIVERSITY was, then, at most a matter of secondary importance in the postwar era. To those who were politically-minded, *university* politics was of no importance at all. Even to the most politically-minded, say to the tiny Communist contingent among the Harvard students at the time, it would have been absolutely inconceivable that the road to revolution or reform could lead through the seizure of a university building or through a demonstration in the college yard. The university, *i.e.,* its students and faculty, was assumed then, as always, to be a promising place for political propaganda, *i.e.,* for gaining political converts; it would not have occurred to anybody that it was a proper or promising place for political action. The very term "university politics" implied something limited and parochial, unrelated to any national issues. For the first few years after World War II the student body was composed largely of veterans. Such students—they gave the tone to the American campuses at the time—were neither unconcerned nor apathetic; in fact, they were quite politically-minded. Having been through the Depression and experienced the war, most of them were keenly interested in avoiding such horrors in the future; they were, in today's parlance, "activists" and "committed." Usually older than the normal student, very often from a very different social milieu than the one which provided the bulk of prewar undergraduates in the leading Eastern universities, the veteran could be expected to be and sometimes was impatient of the classroom routine, parietal regulations, and the social trappings of his education. If there ever was a great generation gap, it certainly existed between those men in their twenties who had been through the war, of the most divergent social and educational background, and the faculty and administration recruited and formed in the then still largely parochial, and to tell the truth, rather stuffy interwar Harvard. Yet, no student rebellion! Even more striking, no widespread alienation, or (as this term really conveys in plain English) boredom and feeling "where-does-it-all-lead." Quite a few people were individually alienated, but instead of blaming it on deans or on our competitive materialistic society and banding together to fight those powers, they dropped out of the college or sought psychiatric help, sometimes in psychoanalysis then just coming into vogue. In fact, there was no one, as yet, to tell those people that they were alienated and the fault was society's. Freudians and neo-Freudians were just beginning their ascent to the commanding heights of the American academic and intellectual community. The popular image of the analyst was not that of a stern prophet decreeing that "modern society dehumanizes its members" or makes them undergo "identity crises," but that of a kindly old man speaking with a German accent who traced all your troubles to something which happened in your childhood and, consequently, could have no conceivable connection with the Defense Department, the Chase Manhattan Bank, or the president of your university.

The student's attitude then was much more individualistic than, as we are led to believe, it is now. You could dislike some—many, most—facets of your college or graduate school existence and still feel that it offered something of value. We did not feel, in regard to the university or society at large, that strange kind of perfectionism which is being inculcated in the young now: either things are perfect, or the whole institution, and the whole society, is utterly wicked. Either you experience a rapturous feeling of Brotherhood, Equality, and Relevance, or the whole thing is a fraud. One did not feel that the place where one studied was the proper place to seek emotional and spiritual fulfillment. It was not a substitute for the church, family or tribe; it was simply a place at which one spent a certain amount of time, with which one identified to a greater or lesser extent, for good or spurious reasons; but it was certainly not some mysterious power exerting some fateful force over one's life.

What was to strike one forcibly during the Columbia troubles in 1968 and the Harvard mess of 1969 was the emotional intensity with which so many assailants and defenders of the university reacted to them. It went far beyond the emotional attachment of one type of alumnus to whom the university is a place where he spent some happy years, or the resentment of another who recalls it as a place where he suffered real or imaginary snubs and unhappiness. It had little to do with the reasonable pride or impatience at one's association with a famous institution. For some, they were storming a citadel of unrighteousness, others bewailed a paradise lost. One felt in the presence of some wild, irrational force. In the past, in some other societies, it had manifested itself in national and religious conflicts. But here in twentieth-century America it swirled around the university, something which in the last analysis is only a collection of people and buildings. It was at once tragic and comical. One felt indignant, then sad, then embarrassed that the unprecedented national effort and investment in education should culminate in such tragic idiocies, that so many distinguished and learned persons, newspapers, and magazines should hurry with explanations, should probe and poke the psychology of the young, and yet not say the obvious: it does not make any sense. For it just didn't, whatever one's

political persuasion, whatever one's view of the merits and
shortcomings of American society. Two things have been
striking about the reaction to various incidents of the above
sort. We have grown accustomed so much to looking for
deeper causes of everything that we fail to consider even the
possibility of *obvious* ones: perhaps—just perhaps—the
primary responsibility for student unrest lies with the
students who cause unrest. Then we have grown so addicted
to moralistic brooding over our society that it has become
unfashionable to credit error, or accident, with any role in
our misfortunes. "Who has sinned?" rather than "who has
goofed?" is the question asked in the case of a tottering
foreign policy or a tottering university.

Here, then, is another disturbing similarity to a totalitarian
society. Every student of Communist China or of the Soviet
Union (though the Russians have grown somewhat better in
this respect recently) knows how hard it is for them to admit
the possibility of error or accident as major elements in
human behavior. A factory which lags in production, an
office which gets bogged down in paper work, an athletic
team which unexpectedly loses—are those simply results of
human imperfectibility, incompetence, or just-one-of-those-
things? Of course not! Someone has failed to absorb the
teachings of Comrade Mao, to show proper respect and
devotion for the people's property, for socialism. We talk a
great deal about the polarization of opinion over student
unrest in America, but this is a superficial judgment. *Almost*
everybody agrees in seeking its source in some *moral* quality
of the young men concerned: they are either "idealists"
(whether misguided or not), or "bums." Few attribute those
phenomena to error, suggestibility or delusion so frequent
among young men of all ages and not uncommon among
their elders.

This enlargement of the area of guilt and virtue found an
amusing illustration in one sequence of the Harvard troubles

of 1969. A faculty committee was formed to define rights and responsibilities of members of the academic community. The committee defined several types of unacceptable behavior on the part of the students. Then it was felt only fair to find some unacceptable (*i.e.,* morally wrong and, presumably, subject to censure and punishment) behavior in the case of a university official. A university administrator, it was declared, had *no right* to remain "insensitive" to reasoned demands by a student group. I forget for how long this interesting new category of moral dereliction was enshrined as such within the regulations. But it reminds one of nothing as much as of the heinous crime often imputed to a disgraced Soviet official: "He has lost touch with the masses . . ."

One might, at this point, launch into a disquisition on Calvinistic morality, and its current rebirth in certain fashionable varieties of Freudianism as practiced by certain politicians, columnists, and television programs. But it is more instructive to revert to our less sophisticated and more liberal university of a generation ago. The student had more freedom. Of course his studies, deportment, etc. were much more regulated than they are now, excessively so in many cases. Yet, apart from some schools with a specific religious orientation, these regulations bore on the student's outward behavior. What is the requirement to wear ties in the classroom, or to take examinations, and so on, compared with the burden of anxiety and moral earnestness which weighs so heavily on so many young men today (and if our moralists had their way would weigh on them all?). The college acknowledged the right of young men and women to by young, hence at times frivolous and irresponsible. Now the Left and the Right in this country, "soft" college administrators as well as the hard line ones, appear to be in a veritable conspiracy to force their charges to care and to worry. Many would extend this tyranny beyond the university to other schools, to professions. Some would transform our whole education from the kindergarten to the graduate school into an orgy of concern, a continuing bull session about "issues," combined with a therapy group in "interacting." In a totalitarian society such regimen has at least a clear-cut purpose and direction, and is not allowed to interfere with formal education, *i.e.,* the acquisition of knowledge. In our own, the result (as we are finding out now) would be people arriving at the threshold of adulthood in a state of exhaustion and confusion, weary of the continuous chatter about the U.N., poverty and environment; seeking an escape in esoteric cults, drugs, violence. Fortunately this is unlikely to become universal: you cannot bore all the people all the time.

AS AGAINST "CONCERN" the old university encouraged curiosity. This sounds rather unsensational until we reflect how seldom we hear today that the encouragement of intellectual curiosity should be the main goal of education. Part of the blame lies in certain unfortunate habits of speech and terminology which prevailed then; which in those far away days seemed quite innocuous, but which were to lead first to a misunderstanding, then to a controversy, and then to trouble. The word "research." It would be much better if this term did not exist and if teachers asked how they employed their time apart from teaching were compelled to say "I am very much interested in finding out how this or that works or what happened, etc." But, even in 1945, research carried a rather cold if not repellent connotation, and recently has almost come to be associated with something anti-social. If you "do" research, it means that you selfishly withhold yourself from the students, from teaching, sit in your cubicle probably learning about something of no use to anyone else, if not indeed doing it for the wicked government and/or industry. An alert, modern social scientist much prefers the word "investigate." *That* carries the connotation of trying to catch somebody (again government, industry, or the establishment academicians) at something they have tried to conceal or distort. But independently of such imputations, the word *is* unfortunate. When it does not have sinister implications, it still tends to smack of something unnatural and strained: a man is doing it for the ignoble reason of making money or because that is his somewhat demeaning job (thus, doing research for a presidential or senatorial speech; why don't we hear of presidents and senators doing research?), or because he wants to be advanced or retained at a university. The idea of research as an unstrained, pleasurable, and (apart from science) potentially useful activity, does not come easily.

Yet all the vast convolutions of this term (and I have not as yet discussed the contentious problem of pure *vs.* applied research) were not so evident or troublesome in the postwar period. To some, indeed, research was a good thing and an honorable activity. In a good university the faculty was interested in research, which, miraculously enough was taken then to mean that they liked what they taught and consequently were interested in finding out more about it. Hence students were attracted to a university like Harvard because the faculty was interested in research, *i.e.,* interested and interesting. Oh, of course there were also snobbish reasons, and also your social mobility and what-have-you. But still I maintain that many of us, undergraduates and graduates, believed that we attended the school we did because we were curious, because we would learn interesting things, eventually do them ourselves, lead interesting, *i.e.,* useful lives. Many, of course, were to be disappointed in their expectations. They would become bored or resentful, or decide that academic life was not for them. But even in most such cases there was usually an appreciation of individual reasons for one's disappointment. Some would seek more active lives outside the university, without necessarily blaming the university for not being what it cannot be. Some would seek a smaller school in preference to a large one. Some would simply resign themselves to a few years of drudgery and then turn their back on the whole thing, without either nostalgia or undue resentment. There was as yet little urge to repair to some fashionable philosopher to find reasons for one's dissatisfaction, to decide that if one was occasionally restless, or bored, it must be the university or society which is at fault.

Few, by the same token, were entirely satisfied with what they were getting. Higher education did involve some drudgery. This, in turn, was an inevitable consequence of the character of the prewar American high school. Today it undoubtedly does its job better, though how long this will last with the spread of moral earnestness and drugs is again open to question. But the old high school had tried to amuse the student too much, to "develop his whole personality," as the phrase went, rather than to insist too strenuously on his learning to write, to deal with foreign languages and master mathematics. The student arrived in college or even the graduate school with his personality properly rounded out, as we then foolishly believed, but without those necessary tools of higher education. It is unexhilarating at best (and to a man in his twenties it can be sheer torture) to learn a language or elementary mathematics. Hence the drudgery. Some would also classify as such the whole business of examinations, attendance at lectures, and the like. But this, again, was a necessary product of the heterogeneity of the American educational system. In the brave new world of today it is proposed to dispense with such relics of the oppressive past. Yet many able and even ambitious people are at the same time indolent. Will they learn languages, mathematics, and the rest, without sanctions and rewards? Examinations remain a clumsy but still a useful way of indicating to the student whether he is applying his energies to the right field, in the right way, and so on. This may be elitism, another cardinal sin in today's educational catechism, but is it not more profitable to listen to a great teacher even in a large lecture course rather than to rap with a lesser one in one of those small intimate discussion groups?

Anyway, to that generation, many of whose members were veterans, sitting and listening to a lecture did not appear unduly oppressive, and the authority exerted by deans, professors and examinations not unduly severe compared with that they had experienced at the hands of sergeants and commanding officers. The certain passivity inherent in the system, the alleged trauma of examinations, could not be taken as excessive or unpleasant compared with certain aspects of their wartime occupations. And so perhaps the moral is that higher education can be appreciated, or by some endured, only after a period of earning one's livelihood (or, anyway, working).

The passion for discussion and participation was not nearly as strong as it is now. Both of course are necessary ingredients of education and have been a distinguishing mark of the Anglo-American tradition. They offered a fortunate contrast to the Continental pattern where, as a general rule, you did have hundreds of students trooping into vast lecture rooms to hear professors recite from their lecture notes, which usually had been printed anyway. But there was no vociferous demand that *all* of education should consist of discussion. The students, after all, felt they were expending time, and sometimes their own money; and perhaps perversely by modern standards, they felt that sometimes they should listen to an authority in the field (elitism, again!) rather than to each other. The idea of student-run courses, so much in vogue nowadays, would have encountered this—to us, startling—objection that students talk and discuss things anyway so why should one pay for it. "Current affairs," even "politics," were the rage. Maybe the university *c.* 1900 was an ivory tower, certainly not the one of 1946. But again does one go to college just to talk and learn what one can read in a newspaper or magazine?

In brief, education, higher education, was looked at as a very ordinary activity, which like many other ordinary activities, can be bad, tolerable, or at times (and, in principle, ought to be) exhilarating. This would be not worth stressing except for the fact that such an attitude toward education appears, alas, to have been exceptional and confined to the period following the war. Both before and currently, education has been regarded as something in the nature of magic. Before it was assumed to be a powerful force shaping one's whole personality: one went to Williams, Virginia, or Harvard, and lo! one remained for the rest of one's life a Williams, etc., man. It was assumed to endow one with special graces, with a new personality; a son of a Jewish or Irish immigrant was transformed into a member of the cultured elite (something which we would today call the Establishment) unless, of course, he was rejected and his whole subsequent life ruined. There was thus a special *mystique* about education centered around but not confined to the Eastern schools, and like every mystique it contained a lot of nonsense as well as a small kernel of truth. Part of the blame could be attributed to bad books and films, many of them amazingly enough not about Williams or Harvard, but about the English public schools, West Point, or Rockne of Notre Dame. A classical tale was that of a young man, uncertain or confused, when suddenly an interview with an understanding coach or dean, a friendly hand on his shoulder, would turn him away from a road to perdition, the life of a wastrel and drunkard, to a sober, useful and profitable career.

From that C. Aubrey Smith-Robert Donat picture of education we have plunged, after a short interval, into one shaped by C. Wright Mills and Herbert Marcuse. The university is no longer a school of character, it is a sausage factory designed to produce obedient and conformist tools for the Establishment. To be sure, there are still bad books and movies, more than before as a matter of fact. That kindly dean who puffed on the pipe while glancing with idiotic benevolence at a young man across the desk has been transformed into a hard-faced official, probably with a private line to the F.B.I. or the Pentagon, trying to dissuade the young idealist from seizing his office. But the dominant stereotypes are fed much more by administrators and sociologists with their investigations and statistics. And, again, for a vast majority of them, even the so-called moderates, education is not and should not be the prosaic business of learning and enjoying various skills and professions. It is a magic which if employed correctly will yet save society and the world; and, if not, will pull them down along with institutions of higher learning. The old mystique had the saving quality of being centered around the individual teacher and student. In the new one you have vast numbers of teachers catering to the vast crowds of students (to be sure, in small groups, as well as students instructing each other, again in small groups), all of them milling around full of indignation and the zeal to remake society, to devise innovative ways of teaching and interacting, to change the quality of life. . . .

Mystique and education do not mix. The troubled young man of yore should have sought help not from the dean or the coach but from a minister, psychiatrist, or an uncle.* And in real life he probably did. The young men and women who are troubled about politics today, which is in itself quite

---

*Coaches and other athletic leaders had been traditionally assumed to be character builders. But this, alongside with similar claims on behalf of marine sergeants and spinster librarians, has not withstood the triumphant advance of analysts and sociologists. Some years ago "Red" Blaik gravely warned that the de-emphasis of football would make

normal and understandable, should then become politically active. *Indirectly* the university, just as every school, ought and often does help its members in their personality problems. If it tries to do so directly it is only asking for trouble, and probably does more harm than good. The same goes for politics.

The reason lies not in the ascription to the university of any unusual function, in viewing it as a temple of learning which ought not to be penetrated by any vulgar noises from the outside. Quite the contrary. The reason must be sought once again in the fact that education is a very prosaic activity and not magic. If at all good, education must possess the qualities of precision and clarity; it must deal for the most part in facts rather than feelings. It is to be hoped, indeed, that technical competence makes for a fuller personality, sometimes for a happier individual, perhaps for one who is more compassionate or creative than he would be without it. But the necessary goal must be that competence, the rest coming, so to speak, as a bonus. Who would exchange a competent doctor for one who, while incompetent, had an impeccable bedside manner as well as a highly developed social conscience? And it is a mistake to think that the goal of undergraduate education can or ought to be drastically different from the professional one: it must be to try to make *every* student know well—to understand thoroughly—*something.* A liberal education seeks to indoctrinate the student in *curiosity;* a totalitarian (a religious) one, in an *attitude.*

SUCH GENERALITIES can be best understood in referring

America's young men like those of France, *i.e.,* interested only in girls. (Had that been all!) More recently, members of the Harvard crew grew their hair long and issued statements on various matters of social importance. They then went to the Olympic Games and were badly defeated. Possibly they would have lost in any case.

to the period when higher education in America became a serious, but not as yet depressing, business. It would be unrealistic to claim that the faculties of colleges and universities, even the leading ones, were in the postwar period composed entirely of authorities in their fields, that the students *en masse* eschewed easy or superficial courses in favor of austerely instructive ones. But in most good American schools the focus of interest shifted from the traditional concept of the popular teacher, *i.e.,* one who was a "character" who just cracked jokes, or exuded friendly and therapeutic influence, to one who was a craftsman in his field. The latter was not necessarily famous, nor in some cases what is known as a productive scholar, but he had something interesting, sometimes amusing, to say.

It is Charles McIlwain who comes most readily to my mind under this rubric. He was to retire from active teaching in 1946, and being already of great age, communication between him and a first-year graduate student could not be easy. His scholarship was of a narrow (some would say pedantic) type. He was far from being a dazzling lecturer, and his field—English constitutional history and earlier political theory—appeared to be of little relevance to the issues and concerns of modern politics. Neither Dr. Marx nor Dr. Freud was summoned to help in the interpretation of the series of long and obscure constitutional documents or medieval and early modern political doctrines. It was, it appeared at first, a dry, legalistic approach which made of figures as colorful as Henry II or Henry VIII just legal innovators, and of events so rich and varied in their background as the Puritan and American Revolutions just struggles between contending constitutional interpretations. Yet soon one realized that he was immersed in genuine historical reality, that by having one's attention focused so well on one vital aspect of it, the student was immeasurably better prepared to understand other aspects and connections than he would have been after a course which dully and cautiously tried to appease every opinion and approach. This proceeded partly from the fascination inherent in tracing a clause or a single word of an old document to its real meaning in a way as intriguing as is the search through real and feigned clues on which a good mystery writer takes his reader. As against many a course in social science from which a student emerges with intellectual indigestion, and the feeling that everything depends on everything else so what is the use, one came from this type of experience with the satisfaction of having grasped something important. Or, if dissatisfied, then with the right kind of dissatisfaction: *because* the argument was so impressive, so genuinely a product of learning and conviction, that one was stimulated to probe again for weak spots, was stimulated to try to improve upon it, to grasp for alternative solutions. One also emerged from McIlwain's courses inoculated against superficiality in approaching history, and against the kind of intellectual argument which consists mainly in bandying names and views of real and alleged authorities. It is insufficient to describe such teaching as challenging; one learned to understand history.

The deep, perhaps prudent, suspicion of learning which has always characterized this society has been responsible for the belief that the student has somehow to be entrapped or scared into it. Hence the vogue at one time of the professor "character": you were entranced or amused by his personality and antics, and lo! before you realized, you learned something. Nowadays the idea is to link the teaching process to "issues." The pupil is to be instructed no longer by being amused but by being made anxious or indignant. Hannibal as a child, we are told, was made to hate the Romans through being compelled by his father to learn Latin. Now we would reverse this process. Hence the popularity in certain pedagogical circles of the idea of little workshops instructing in the iniquities of American imperialism, pollution, and male chauvinism; is this not the most efficacious way of making the youth of today interested in economics, environment, and sociology?

The amusement approach may be exemplified by the parable of Russian history employed by a professor who will remain nameless. You have the eternal Russian peasant drowsing on the stove. Suddenly his slumber is interrupted; seized by an incomprehensible access of energy he scrambles down (few could understand how one could sleep on the stove but it only added to the inherent mystery of the subject), and flings himself into a wild dance. And then his energy and passion are drained. He grows weary. Back to the stove. There you had the tragic sense of Russian history.

For all the enhanced interest in things Russian and Soviet after World War II there was a real danger that most of the money and effort expended on new programs of study and research institutes would be misdirected. Such efforts, it appeared, might throw only a cloak of academic respectability over the peasant stove and what was soon to become known as the "Kremlinological" approaches: teachers and students would be immersed in the discussion of the Russian soul throughout the ages, or contrariwise, "What will the Russians do next." The rapidly advancing field of social psychology threatened to reinforce the peasant-stove school: weren't Russians *very tightly* swaddled throughout their infancy, but at times completely unwrapped, thus making for long periods of repression punctured by episodes of wild anarchic freedom? We were saved from such extravagances and stultifying stereotypes very largely through the presence in the academic world then of a veritable handful of distinguished scholars in the field of Russian history. They had been teaching and writing for some time, of course, but it is now in this educational emergency that they exerted crucial and beneficial influence. The stove-climbers and swaddlers beat a retreat, constrained in many cases to turn their skills to analyzing American society. The budding Kremlinologists were put in their place, which often and quite properly turned out to be the C.I.A. Scholarship prevailed.

One of the handful was Professor Michael Karpovich of Harvard. Those who studied directly under him would undoubtedly credit Karpovich with much more than just saving Russian studies from the faults of false exoticism and excessive utilitarianism. His very personality exemplified and emanated some of the best characteristics of the pre-revolutionary Russian intelligentsia, a deep impression of civilized humanity and intellectual liveliness, a strong liberal bias yet free of that dogmatism which made so many Russian intellectuals of that period go astray (in a manner reminiscent, alas, of so many of our own). His favored field was that of nineteenth-century Russian intellectual history, and it is no accident that this field was to flourish in American scholarship of the last twenty years. Few large areas of a foreign culture have become so firmly a part of the American academic idiom as that involved and entrancing story. It required great erudition and firm intellectual balance to guide both the future specialist and the general student safely through a subject so full of pitfalls of false enthusiasm and facile generalization, to see its organic connection with, at the same time as significant differences from, the general current of Western culture. It was a Russia vastly more complex yet at the same time more understandable than that of the popularizer who has peopled it almost exclusively with Rasputins, Grand Dukes, and revolutionaries. Again one feels that the value of this unhurried, unsensational approach transcended its benefits to the future writer of a doctoral dissertation, or a non-specialist's enhanced pleasure in reading a Russian novel. One learned to understand a great nation and its tragic history in a way that no recital of political facts and economic statistics could furnish by itself. And quite beyond and apart from Russia, one learned *to understand,* which is what education is all about.

THE PHANTOM OF RELEVANCE which we are supposed to worship today has a companion with the somewhat awkward name of Challenging the Traditional Beliefs and Values. To be sure, this has become rather difficult, for in true American fashion yesterday's dissent has come close to being today's conformity. Who is truly alienated? One who says he is, or one who thinks himself to be part of the mainstream of American culture but who cannot find a book to read, a film or a play to attend, or sometimes even a tailor to minister to his allegedly non-conformist tastes? The meaning of non-conformity has become hazy and confined; and soon those young intellectuals, with their not uncommon propensity to stress their difference from the common herd and to incur *mild* martyrdom, will be constrained to risk their academic or professional advancement and their social acceptance by proclaiming at cocktail parties that there is no generation gap and that Vice-President Agnew may not be entirely wrong!

In yonder times of which I write, non-conformity still had something of its original and rather bracing meaning. Yes, there were Marxists and even Communists on the faculties of American universities, soon to become the object of interest and pursuit by the congressional committees, and of the type of reprobation by the media of mass communication which is now reserved for the non-sensitive, non-communicating-with-the-youth college officials and parents. The Communists were, of course, not real non-conformists. They were simply what might be described as geographically misplaced conformists, *i.e.,* professing in New York or in Cambridge, Massachusetts, views and ideas which were desirable and appreciated in Moscow or Minsk. For a real non-conformist, the type which is very essential on every university scene, I offer the example of Professor Joseph Schumpeter.

At first such a characterization may appear absurd. Here was one of the most famous economists of his era, renowned even before World War I. High academic preferments in Europe, as well as a brief and rather unfortunate stint as Austria's minister of finance, preceded Schumpeter's arrival at the Harvard Economics Department. His vivacity and his equally Viennese non-reticence about his social and intellectual achievements would appear to make such characterization even more absurd.

Schumpeter was a non-conformist somewhat in the manner of the man who when asked to join Free-Masonry replied that he could not for two reasons: he was a Catholic and he did not believe in God. Schumpeter did not believe in Keynesian economics, then already in ascendancy in academic and government circles. In fact, on both economic and sociological grounds, he viewed the great English economist's approach as incorrect and unpractical. He was a strong exponent of the classical school of political economy to which he made distinct contributions. Yet he did not believe that capitalism could be saved or mended.

A book which at the time stirred up a great deal of interest and controversy was Friedrich von Hayek's *Road to Serfdom*. It was a spirited argument on behalf of market economy as against the encroachments and (as the author believed) false premises and promises of the welfare state, which shortly became enthroned with the victory of the Labour Party in Great Britain. A strictly regulated economy was bound to bring a demise of the traditional liberties of the West or, at best, the "muddle of the middle," a society with some of the defects yet without the main benefits of either authoritarianism or liberal democracy. What was needed, Hayek believed, was a firm reaffirmation of the traditional values of liberalism, among them that of free enterprise.

Schumpeter, before his students, professed his incredulity

at Hayek's conclusion. How could a fellow Austrian, a man of his own generation and intellectual and social background, *still* believe that the trend could be reversed, that capitalism, hence liberalism, could be saved? Schumpeter himself had no doubt that on all possible grounds the liberal economic system was supremely desirable and the only possible basis for a free and progressive society, for international collaboration and peace. But the almost inevitable trend was the other way. Social and psychological underpinnings of that beneficent system were being knocked out, and a democracy would not cling to it simply because it was *demonstrably* superior on rational grounds to any alternative. What was in the offing was socialism of one sort or another. Yet, in whatever form, it would not offer the humanitarian and economic benefits its proponents envisaged. Most likely the socialist states of the future would tend to be authoritarian rather than democratic, militaristic rather than peace-loving. In brief, a less dramatic and masochistic version of Orwell's *1984*.

Some of those prophecies and fears appear today uncomfortably close to the facts. Some have, fortunately, been dispelled, at least so far as the West is concerned. The jury is still out on the most fundamental conclusions and prophecies of both Schumpeter and Hayek. Besides his professional judgment, it was easy to see in Schumpeter's sardonic vision of the future, though advanced without any bitterness or passion, a strong sympathy for a "more civilized world," that before 1914, for the elegance and graces epitomized by Vienna of a bygone era. Yet it was not mere nostalgia or a cultured European's slighting of the allegedly barbarous Americans. He admired the strength and vigor of his adopted country: the war had been won in the main by the prodigious performance of the American economy. His civilized pessimism was a useful and challenging antidote to the already ascendant point of view that social and economic planning could perform miracles. Strong (and as against the Keynesian persuasion, unorthodox) views did not make Schumpeter intellectually intolerant. He was an understanding advocate of those younger economists who, unfashionable in a different way, clung to Marx's economic apparatus. He relished intellectual dispute, conveyed the feeling that it should be conducted with wit and culture rather than with pompous evocation of alleged eternal verities and social priorities. Economics appeared not as a dismal but an elegant and graceful science.

Other names could be cited, yet the three I have given convey much of the flavor of education at Harvard, and undoubtedly at many other leading universities in the America of the time. There were other excellent teachers, some more popular with the students, some much better known outside the academic world. There were also teachers who were just competent and/or dull. There were also, as there are bound to be, windbags, people superficial in their lectures, shabby in their scholarship; and worst of all, there were already lecturers who were both superficial and popular. Yet the tone of the place of academic life in general, was set in the type of concerns and approach which emanated from the men I spoke of (at least insofar as the area of the social sciences is concerned, though I am pretty sure a student of humanities or science of the period could offer similar examples for a similar lesson). But the fact that they were in the social sciences, the area which was to grow inordinately, probably excessively, in popularity as the field of study for undergraduates and graduates alike, underscores the contrast between then and now. Students today are supposed to take courses of current and pressing interest and importance and to seek out young and dynamic instructors with whom they can communicate. Those three were certainly not young, could not (with the exception of Schumpeter) be described as dynamic as the term is currently understood; the difference of age and background interposed a barrier to that close communication and frequent contact which is supposed to be of such great importance in education. They were certainly courteous, easily approachable and helpful, but would have been devoid of that impulse that has of late prompted many an elderly and sometimes a distinguished professor to embrace vociferously what he conceives to be the cause of youth. A certain degree of distance does not imply lack of sympathy, often quite the contrary; respect for accomplishment and age is not a sign of repression but of maturity and a civilized mind.

TO REPEAT, this was not the golden age of the American university but what could then be viewed, with some justification, as a promise of one. One could hope for—and one did see—a rapid diminution of snobbery, stuffiness and prejudice which had afflicted the Eastern academic establishment. The university was emerging from a period of penuriousness, shedding both its parochialism and the inferiority complex vis-à-vis the European models. The current, often choleric, dispute as to whether those were Good or Bad Old Days, like all such exercises, misses the point. Because we deplore the new evils does not mean that we long for the old ones any more than by being opposed to pollution we want to bring back the conditions when tuberculosis and polio were widespread. And so the real choice is not between the turbulence, agitation, and violence on today's campuses and yesterday's apparent detachment from society's problems, its preoccupation with fraternities, sororities, and clubs. The alleged apathy of the student of those days is very largely a myth, unless by it is meant the absence of that current neurosis, indeed at times psychosis, which colors today's college life: the feelings of guilt and boredom which together add up to despondency were not as yet stamped upon a significant portion of the younger generation, because as yet there were no persistent voices excusing, encouraging and extolling such sentiments, because a sizeable element of the intellectual community was not as yet ready to see excitement as evidence of idealism. The question is, then, why so many people then young were to become in their middle age baffled and confused, why so many of them as teachers, administrators, public figures of one sort or another have shown themselves weak or credulous or both, incapable or unwilling to see forthcoming danger, helpless in the face of clear and present ones? Why did the people whose own education was sound fail to spot serious flaws in the educational practices and attitudes which were to grow in the intervening period and which are responsible for so many of the troubles of the last few years?

Here, again, if we start talking about industrialized society, the crisis of values, the Vietnam War, and the like, the picture becomes blurred. Without ignoring those, it is more helpful to return the focus to the university, to refer to one's own impressions and experiences.

2

America's
Cultural Revolution

OUR RELUCTANCE, which has assumed the proportions of a national affliction, to credit intelligence (or the lack of it) with a major responsibility for the course of events has also colored our thinking about the crisis in our higher education. To say that we find ourselves in the present mess because so many of our college administrators and teachers have been foolish, or unrealistic, immediately encounters a violent protest from the believers in Deeper Causes. "Ah...," they exclaim, "but what are the socio-cultural factors which made them so?" That, to be sure, is an important and interesting question, just as it is important for medicine to seek the psychological and social reasons *why* a man becomes an alcoholic or drug addict. But a doctor does not postpone an attempted cure until those deeper and interesting causes and problems have been identified and solved.

What are those "deeper causes"? Has there been somewhere along the road a fatal turn which has brought us to our present troubles? Or has there been a slow accretion of mistakes: of growing insensitivity to the students' real needs and feelings, to the community in which the given school is located, to society at large?

To get a handle on those vast and rather vague questions one might, first of all, address oneself to the query whether, and how, the American university has been discharging its proper function, that of contributing to learning and producing educated men and women, with (insofar as the graduate schools are concerned) requisite professional skills. Here the first phenomenon which strikes us is the apparent and huge paradox. In statistical terms the whole enterprise appears to have been a huge success. One can employ such criteria as the nationality of Nobel Prize winners since the war to see how American science has in practically every major field dominated the world-wide picture. It is unreasonable to attribute it *just* to the great wealth of the country. Certainly the already much richer and technologically more advanced America had not enjoyed that superiority over Germany, France and Britain between 1900 and 1940 that it has in recent years when those countries have largely recovered from the war. Somewhat similar has been the growth and international influence of American scholarship in non-scientific fields. Here there are also important contributory factors in the influx to the United States of the refugees in the 1930s, and in the continuing "brain drain" from Europe after the war, and in superior material resources. Whatever the reasons, the achievement of the American educational institutions is undeniable.

Insofar as teaching is concerned, the record of the U.S. colleges and universities has been equally impressive. Higher education has been rendered accessible to almost anybody with a modicum of ability whatever qualifications on account of race, financial resources, etc. One can adduce only the ill-informed would question the enormous progress in this respect since 1945, a national performance unparalleled in history, in making higher education so widespread—and, again, whatever reservations one may feel called upon to make, so much better than it used to be.* Few, again, would question that the technical levels of proficiency have risen in all professions, just as the general fare offered the college student is much richer, and (with the exceptions we shall discuss) more solid than a generation ago.

And yet the paradox is obvious. Somehow this superior education must be felt of lesser importance to their lives by the current generation of students; their enjoyment of it less intense. Otherwise *they* would not tolerate the current turbulence and interruptions. It is obviously *not* the very small minority of "activists" or "radicals" who have been responsible for our schools being in the sad condition they are in. It is the great majority who go about their studies, and yet somehow must fail to feel them of sufficient importance, for otherwise how could they tolerate those conditions? The same holds true of the faculties: the number of actual trouble-makers or "radicals" is small and, just as in the case of students, no greater than in the quiet times. But the great majority must have become confused and uncertain of themselves. Otherwise, how could a man who believed English literature or physics to be of sufficient importance to devote his life to them, fail to realize that learning and teaching have to be protected, for they can flourish only in a civilized setting. Had learning been considered of great importance by the people engaged in it, not to mention society at large, not even the wretched Vietnam war could have been allowed to inflict this national calamity on our institutions of higher learning. It would have been seen by the .nass of teachers and students alike that it is just as illogical and impermissible to

---

*We shall not, however, employ the silly cliché that the present generation of students is the best educated ever. Of course it is, but every successive generation of students in the last few hundred years has found itself the recipient of more advanced knowledge than the preceding one.

disrupt the functioning of a university on account of some real or alleged sins and faults of our government as it would be that of a hospital—that students and teachers may and even ought to become passionately involved in politics, but universities must not. Institutions are strong and resilient mainly insofar as the people connected with them feel that what they are doing is worthwhile and important, and hence must not be given up or disparaged even in the face of personal or national anxiety. Some twenty years ago one could feel that the American university was on its way to becoming a major American contribution to history. A blend of the English and Continental traditions yet quite distinct from its prototype, more ambitious (yet reasonably so) in its claims of educating the individual and influencing society, it promised to stamp its unique mark on society, to become a world-wide force for liberalism in the benevolent sense of this word, and a source of justifiable emulation by other countries.

Today such hopes must appear as a mockery. The university is in the center of public attention, a central institution of national life but in quite a different sense than it had promised to be. When not actually paralyzed or a battleground, it has been at best severely crippled. It has become a theatre where every major drama or tragi-comedy of national life is being performed, where many of the obscurantist tools and forms of agitation have gained a foothold. To be sure, most of the ordinary and useful activities of the university still go on; most of the teachers and students still go about their business. But one has the unhappy feeling that it is like a ship which has lost part of its steering mechanism—instead of pursuing a set course, it keeps turning around. The crew and the passengers *keep* arguing about various desirable directions, but there is little inclination to restore the central mechanism.

RESPECT FOR LEARNING has not grown apace with the great prosperity of American education. Here, perhaps, has been the main source of trouble. No sooner did the somewhat incredulous country, and with it the institutions of higher education, realize the pleasant fact that the end of World War II was not being followed by a period of depression for the former and hence a continuation of penury for the latter, than the question was posed: Education for What?

A small and yet somehow disturbing phenomenon was the discussion in the post-war years of the problem of general education. On the surface the issue was quite sensible and the discussion in the postwar years of the problem of general as having contained some disturbing undertones.

At Harvard, where the discussion originated, it turned first around the character of undergraduate curriculum. It was argued quite cogently that some students were in danger of having their undergraduate education too one-sided and over-specialized. Under the usual dispensation, the student was expected to "concentrate," *i.e.,* to take a large proportion of his courses in one subject. Considerations of his future graduate career would often tend to make his college studies one-sided; a future doctor or scientist might emerge from college with just a smattering of humanities and social studies. Then his curiosity about other fields could be constrained by the apprehension that if he ventured out of chemistry into classics or history he would be competing with students who had a special preparation and were specializing in those subjects, hence the danger to his grades, general standing, etc. It was, therefore, proposed and enacted, still quite sensibly, to have a core of "general education" courses, quite broad and non-specialized in their character, which would be required of the undergraduate. People with humanistic interests and talents would be

required to take some course in the scientific method which
would not torture them with equations and other recondite
tools of science and yet give them an inkling of how the
scientists live and think. A man who cared little about
anything but mathematics would still be required to become
acquainted with trends and developments of Western
civilization, and yet not forced to memorize dates, battles
and other appurtenances of a "specialized" history course.
And so on.

Educational reform is, of course, a proper concern of an
educational institution; periodic changes in the curriculum
are often a necessity. Many European schools had in the past
deteriorated by allowing their curriculum as well as teaching
methods to ossify, nineteenth-century Oxford and Cambridge
being notable examples. The hustling, "innovative" (as we
would call it today) spirit of the American university has,
then, a good deal to be said for it. Yet what was somewhat
disturbing was the intensity with which this rather humdrum
question was discussed. "General education" was hailed by
its proponents as a veritable and beneficial revolution in
American education, a staggering blow against the old fogies
for whom the educational process consisted in learning more
and more about less and less. Some of its opponents saw, on
the contrary, a sacrilegious blow at the tradition of
scholarship, and a commitment to dilettantism. Immature
and ill-prepared young men and, on the other hand, elderly
professors who have lost their zest for and capacity to pursue
research, would be regaling the students with vague generalities on subjects of which they had but superficial knowledge.
In brief, there was a vast exaggeration of the importance of
the whole question, and insufficient realization that the most
important problem about the university still remained,
always, the same: recruitment of teachers committed to
learning and of students who would respect and appreciate

learning. Compared to it, other problems connected with the university might be important but are still secondary.

Underlying the discussion was the issue I have mentioned before—the false dichotomy between the teacher and the researcher: one giving his all to the student, the other selfishly and sinfully devoting his time to some "narrow" specialty. The main criteria which governed the selection of a man to a permanent professorial position at Harvard, just as at other leading universities, concerned his contribution to his field of knowledge. This often became translated into the brutal question of whether he had "published" or not; and if so, whether in sufficient quantity. Yet, in fact, in better schools the maxim of "publish or perish" was a myth rather than reality. Common sense urged, and discriminating people entrusted with appointments followed it, that such mechanical criteria were fallible and unfair, that publishing could be but one measure of a man's suitability—though his inability to add anything new and interesting to the body of knowledge in his field, even though he might have published many volumes, created a strong presumption of his unsuitability. This undercurrent of bitterness between the "publishers" and those who felt, whether realistically or not, that their concern for and exertion on behalf of the students left them no time or energy for writing and researching colored the dispute about general education. The human problem involved was real and sometimes agonizing, just as was (and especially is today) the problem of the student who though capable and well prepared is too distraught or disturbed to follow his studies.

Yet, in fact, the danger has always threatened from the other side, not that learning and the far from synonymous with it criteria of "publishing" would be emphasized *too much* but *too little*. It would be grotesque to suppose that the faculties of our universities, even the very best of them, have been crowded with people who are giants of productive scholarship, that a ceaseless flow of monographs and scientific papers emerges from every study or laboratory at Berkeley, Columbia, or Harvard. Equally foolish to suppose that in those allegedly careless days most of the students in those institutions spent all their time at studies striving to become budding Einsteins or Keyneses. Far from it. Nor would it have been particularly desirable had such been the case. Why, then, was the discussion about general education disturbing? Because it was a small inkling of what was to become a source of major trouble: a feeling of guilt on the part of the university that it is *just* a university, *i.e.,* an institution centered around learning, rather than something else, or more an institution devoted to character building, to eradicating all of society's evils, a school of idealism, etc.

Typical of this confusion, and even more revealing and disturbing in its implications, was the debate which agitated the faculty and administration some years later. It turned on the nature of qualifications for admission to Harvard College—but, again, reflected similar discussions and dilemmas at other schools. Should a prospective student be judged mainly (few would have said exclusively) by intellectual criteria, *i.e.* his native ability and the level of his preparation? Common sense urges yes. You do not want to be rigid or dogmatic in such matters but, in general, how can the average student enjoy and profit by his studies unless he is well prepared and capable? But there was vociferous dissent. Isn't the function of institutions like Harvard to train national leaders? And how many of such past, and presumably also future, leaders would qualify under the entrance requirements of the College Boards? Could (and this was supposed to be a crushing argument) young Winston Churchill make the freshman class of 1950?

But this is precisely the point. It would be difficult to argue that Churchill was frustrated in his life or handicapped in his historic role by not having gone to Oxford or Cambridge; one suspects the opposite. The American republic has managed well until the very recent years, with but a small proportion of its top leaders being alumni of prestigious universities. It is an unwarranted and wrong-headed elitist assumption that all future men of prominence, whatever their interest and preparation, can be identified and caught at an early age and confined in a few institutions of higher learning.

There is a ready rejoinder that the traditional criteria for college admission have favored those with superior economic status who have been able to procure superior pre-college education. But this, then, is an excellent argument for improving the quality of public education at the pre-college level, something which is unlikely to be accomplished if universities which must provide personnel for that education become confused and lax about their own standards. Or, if one wants to carry the argument to its logical conclusion, the inequality in inherited wealth should be severely restricted. But how can a university help society by becoming less of a university?

The same holds for a variant of the above argument. In today's world, unlike that of fifty or even twenty years ago, college (perhaps even a graduate degree) is a necessity for a well-paid job, for social mobility; hence the need for more education at the college level. This is indeed a crucial problem facing every advanced industrial society. But those who would try to solve it by filling up universities on the basis and in the name of various social needs confuse two things: what the educational system, and society as a whole, must attempt to do, and what the university can and ought to accomplish. Certainly with shortened working hours, with the new opportunities for instruction through television and other advances in technology, there are considerable opportunities for people so motivated to make up their educational deficiencies while holding a job, and *then* attend college. Indeed there is no reason why, if the idea of higher education on a mass scale is held as an imperative for our society, it should be tied up exclusively with a four-year university stint. We could explore various schemes of adult education, and even combine it with industrial labor as has been done in some Communist countries. Finally, some people, many people, are obviously happier and better off if they don't have a college degree. If that conclusion is deemed "undemocratic," then one should not stop at half-way measures and have the courage to adopt the proposal of a Harvard professor around the turn of the century: Congress should pass a law that a Bachelor of Arts degree be conferred on every American citizen upon his birth.

The discussion revealed some anti-intellectual undertones as well as some overly intellectual ones. The university was not encouraging the development of the "whole person" in its students, claimed some. Others implied that it was sinful and a significant measure of the failure of the admissions policy that *all* Harvard students did not have perfect academic records. The discussion, as all academic discussions of those days, was still good-humored; but an initiate into the faculty ranks could already be struck by a rather strong dogmatism on both sides of the debate, and how little inclination there was in this assembly of eminent intellectuals to appeal to *just* common sense.

The American university—it was some years after World War II—was growing prosperous and, like most prosperous men and institutions, taking this prosperity for granted. What did a Democratic politician say after the election of General Eisenhower in 1953? "We have run out of poor people." The growth and prosperity of the American universities led to a spectacular increase in the number and significance of the tribe of college administrators. Sang an academic band: *"silently behind screens multiply the ranks of academic deans. . ."* In the old days of penury there used to be a small core of administrators, many of them professors performing their deaconic functions on a part-time basis, lower adminis- trative functions often discharged by graduate students. Now there grew a distinctive corps of administrators for whom student affairs, various proliferations of university affairs, were a full-time occupation. Inevitably they tended to emphasize that aspect of university life, tried to enhance their function within the organization. It would be unfair to picture the situation in the late 1940s and '50s in terms of any class conflict or clash between the administrator and the professor. On the contrary, the relations between the two groups were as a rule friendly; the faculty as a rule was only too glad that the growth of the administrative side of university life did not put an undue burden on their own time. Nor was there any snobbish stigma attached to work in the non-academic side of the university. There was a realistic and non-condescending recognition of the fact that the job of dealing with student organizations could be as important to the life of the institution as the work performed by a distinguished scholar and teacher. But no more!

Yet it was a disturbing phenomenon. The mere quanti- tative growth of the administrative class, and it was especially great in the state universities, was a significant warning sign that the university was growing too big and complex, and that it was trying to do too much. It was already beginning its well-meant but fatal attempt to do too much for the student, to surround him with advisers and psychiatrists and the like. Those responsible for it were losing sight of that important distinction between the high school and college, that the latter's responsibility for the student's development must be mainly in the intellectual sphere. University years should be a period of freedom. That freedom is not encroached upon by regulations concerning college life, dress, etc., as much as by the intolerable (to most young men and women) feeling that they are watched and surrounded with suffocating solicitude whether by their parents or their deans. The college drifted insensibly into the position of an indulgent parent rather than a school for young adults. It protected its charges from responsibility for minor criminal acts such as shoplifting. In the beginning of the drug craze it tried to deal with it within its own precincts and largely through exhortation. Nothing was better meant but more lamentable in its impact than the vast expansion of the services of psychological counselling and psychiatric treatment for students. Such facilities should exist, and in this day should be financed by the university. But why should they be *within* the university?

The momentum of all that administrative psychological solicitude was to build the illusion that a university was not just a collection of teachers and buildings but some vast and all-intrusive force in its students' lives, a Big Brother watching solicitously and oppressively over their well-being. When the explosion of student unrest came in the late 1960s, it was evident that quite apart from Vietnam, and any other political issues, a strong element in it was hostility to the university as such. Small wonder!

HERE I MUST DISCLAIM, for fear of misunderstanding, any intention of seeing the ideal university just as a temple of learning, a collection of classrooms where students gather to listen in reverent awe to *Herr Professor*. It has been a splendid feature of English and American universities to make college more than just a place of instruction, a place where sports, social and political activities of all sorts should be encouraged. Encouraged, *yes*—but required and run by the school: *no.* * True that the wholesome influence of athletics in

---

*It is regrettable that, unlike in England, sports in American colleges are not run by the students, but by a branch of the college bureaucracy.

keeping young men's minds from undue preoccupation with sex and politics has been much exaggerated, still it may have had something to do with making the American student less interested, in politics at least, than his counterpart in Paris or Calcutta.* It is only a sourpuss who for any reasons would begrudge old college life what there was in it of gaiety, interest in sports, and other pleasurable diversions and that civilized scepticism about over-seriousness in studies or politics.

That scepticism did not indicate lack of interest in politics any more than it implied disrespect for learning. If words are to be used properly, the average student and the academic community in 1950 were not any less concerned about politics than was the case in 1970. It is simply that this interest did not then take the form of what is described today as "activism" (but is quite often a kind of religious frenzy). Issues connected with Henry Wallace's Progressive Party, with the U.S. policy toward China, were discussed quite freely and sometimes passionately. Radical opinions, one would guess, were held then by as large a proportion of Harvard graduate and undergraduate students as now. Radicalism was quite fashionable.

To be sure, this was not the radicalism which expresses itself through noisy demonstrations, seizures of buildings and non-negotiable demands, or at least through certain characteristics of dress and demeanor. Radicalism need not mean exhibitionism. The Old Left, even its extreme Stalinist wing, was rational, if not for the most part reasonable, in its

---

*This notion was evident in the recommendation of an official American mission to Russia shortly before the Bolshevik Revolution. The Russian Army (then in a state of decomposition) was badly in need of an organization like the Y.M.C.A.—organized games, etc.—it gravely opined. And it is only too true that Lenin, contrary to the injunction laid down in Sir Henry Newbolt's little poem (repeatedly and falsely attributed to Grantland Rice), cared whether *he* won or lost rather than "how you played the game."

premises: a revolution under American conditions could not be accomplished or furthered through aimless disturbances and terrorism. A radical party had the need of discipline and organization, of appealing to rather than alienating the mass of population. The universities were places for propaganda and recruitment of new members. Hence it would not have occurred to the most radical student that seizure of an administrative office, or screaming obscenities at elderly deans, could have the slightest connection with advancing the interests of the Fatherland of Socialism, or of the American Communist Party. One must not become too nostalgic for those clean-shaven and respectful young men who were Communists in those days. They had all sorts of unpleasant ideas of what they would do with reactionaries including those in universities *after* they took over power. But until then they would not attack or injure a university for, like an industrial corporation, it was a valuable property to be preserved undamaged for the people, *i.e.,* the Communists, once they took over. To damage it, to interrupt its functioning, was as unthinkable as to desecrate the American flag: why only a *provocateur,* a Trotskyite, would do that!

Communism, then, in the academic community was hardly a problem, unthinkable as a serious danger either to the university or to the republic. Indeed what little there was of it appeared in the late 1940s and '50s to be on the way out, and its decline was not due to persecution but to a combination of revulsion and ridicule. An out-and-out Communist had, of course, to stand up for the Soviet Union, and in those days in view of what the Soviet Union was doing in Eastern Europe, in view of Korea and the internal depredations of Stalinism, only the most inveterate fanatic could defend the Fatherland of Socialism, go on to assert that it was South Korea which attacked the North, and to repeat the old chestnuts about the workers' state. The handful of professors and intellectuals who had been drawn to Mr.

Henry Wallace's Progressive crusade recoiled in the wake of the fiasco of the whole enterprise and the realization that they, just as the likeable former vice-president, had been duped. Most of all, the arguments about the iniquity of American society as against that presided over by Stalin were bound to be greeted with hilarity by even a radically-minded college audience. On the campus, just as in the country at large, Communism appeared to be an insignificant relic of the hectic days of the 1930s, its few devotees among students and faculty useful reminders of how dogmatism can blind people to reality, strip them of any sense of humor and proportion. One could look confidently to the rise of a more mature and sensible type of radicalism. It would attack the real ills of society but from democratic premises and without the morbid need to worship false gods. One had the heartening example of the American labor movement which, in a few years since the war, had managed through its own exertions and without prying congressional committees to shake off the undue influence of Communists and their fellow travellers.

This progress toward greater political maturity within both the intellectual community and the country at large was, alas, checked and largely undone by McCarthyism. One may venture the opinion that the future rise of the New Left was made largely possible by this brief but disastrous interlude when the antics of the senator from Wisconsin and *his* fellow travellers occupied the center of national attention. Unreasonable radicalism—those early Communist affiliations which their holders by this time preferred to forget, or felt genuinely embarrassed about—was, through this combination of publicity and chicanery and sometimes real persecution, rescued from oblivion and ridicule and covered with an aura of martyrdom, or at least a certain romance. The academic community as a whole felt a genuine grievance that, along with the government agencies, where at least such procedures could have some superficial justification, it was subjected to suspicion, prying into its members' past, oaths of loyalty, etc. It was recognized quite correctly that underneath the veneer of search for "subversion," there was a real rebirth of anti-intellectualism, of the attitude that because a man earned his living through teaching or other intellectual pursuits this made him automatically more suspect, liable to be watched more closely than say a lawyer or doctor, *almost* as much as a State Department official. The notion which finally seemed to gain ground as one of the valuable by-products of World War II days—that a professor was *just* like anybody else, not more or less eccentric, not more or less patriotic or dependable—now again was challenged. A wound was inflicted upon the intellectual community which seemingly was closed by the late 1950s, but was too readily reopened in the late '60s.

McCarthyism has quite undeservedly and incorrectly been classified as a kind of conservatism. It was, in fact, a kind of populism. Had the term Establishment been in use at the time it would have described precisely the target of the senator's attack, the object of prejudice and suspicion his speeches and hearings before his committee were intended to fan. Parallels to what was to take place some fifteen years later were quite striking. Just as an official's or professor's membership, even if many years before, in a Marxist discussion group was taken as evidence of his corruption and presumptive treason, so more recently young radicals and their middle-aged mentors sought to draw similar conclusions from a professor's association with the government of the United States either as an official or a consultant. McCarthy popularized the notion of the plot—some vague but vast conspiracy, the threads of which run from the classroom through Washington offices to countries in the Far East, crumbling before Communism, aided and abetted by treason. This plot was to reappear as one of the more absurd versions of the misdeeds of the military-industrial complex: at the instigation of Wall Street, and with the help of servile academicians, it aims to enslave people abroad, as well as repress the poor at home. There are, of course, major differences. McCarthy's was very much a one-man show, though there were some would-be imitators and henchmen of the senator from Wisconsin. The present trouble is much, much more widespread and cannot be attributed to one person or group. McCarthyism was but a vulgar episode in American politics; the senator, rather unwisely from his point of view, failed to equip himself with a philosophy and to procure a political base. Here, again, the movement of protest, dissent, the New Left, or what-have-you has reached more deeply and widely and has posed a fundamental challenge to America's institutions.

This distinction sometimes tends to become blurred for the mythology of ritualistic liberalism has at times elevated McCarthyism to a threat to democracy comparable to that of Hitler's. That view, in turn, was quite naturally adopted and expanded by left-wing and anti-American circles in Britain and France to the point where a casual reader of one of their newspapers or magazines might well conclude that between 1950 and 1954 the U.S. had large-scale concentration camps for political dissidents and that the senator, rather than just presiding over a subcommittee of the U.S. Senate for two years, was in fact the directing spirit of the whole American government.

In the U.S.A. and within the academic community there was also some tendency to exaggerate the extent of the threat and of the actual damage. One story may be instructive on this count. Among my acquaintances at Harvard at the time was a young and enterprising instructor with no pronounced political interests or affiliations. Sometime in the 1950s he was given a large and prestigious fellowship to study abroad. He then settled down and pursued his academic career in Britain. It then came as a distinct shock to myself as well as to other people who knew him in his graduate student days to read, many years later, an article by him in a left-wing English publication where he discussed political repression in the U.S. and proceeded to identify himself with quiet pride as one of its victims! To be sure, such a reputation was *then* not likely to hurt him in England and in his profession. It is pleasant to add that the young man in question has evidently forgiven his country, has come back, and now occupies quite a remunerative academic position!

In 1958 McCarthyism seemed well in the past: universities and professors were not being investigated or accused. In fact, the torpor of the Eisenhower era appeared to have pervaded them as well as society as a whole. I remember discussing this phenomenon with a distinguished and deservedly very popular member of the Harvard Law School, a man of impeccable liberal credentials. He lapsed into thoughtful silence, and then put down his martini glass with some violence, spilling his drink: "I almost miss McCarthy," he said. *"Something* was going on."

To be honest about it, McCarthyism failed to rouse much protest or even interest among the students. Reasons for it may be sought in alleged apathy of that generation, but there were probably two main causes for that attitude. First, as far as the attack on the universities was concerned, its intense phase was rather brief: it extended from the winter of 1953 when McCarthy, on becoming chairman of that sub-committee, could embark on his antics, to the spring of 1954. Then came the famous televised hearings of McCarthy plus the Cohn-and-Schine embroglio with the Army and, when a sly Boston lawyer outplayed the senator, McCarthy's charm, if this be the proper word, was definitely broken and he then started on his rapid decline.

Apart from this short span, the other and perhaps basic

reason was that young people are temperamentally more prone to attack rather than to defend established institutions. It is only now that we are beginning to have vague stirrings of a students' movement to *defend* universities, though there can be no doubt that all along the number of those opposed to riots, takeovers, etc. has far exceeded those who engaged in them or who approved of such activities. Last but not least, there were a lot of people under, as well as over, thirty who were scared. Not so much (especially where the young were concerned) in the vulgar sense of the word—of the consequences of taking a principled opposition to the activities of the exhibitionist from Appleton, Wisconsin—as in the sense of being afraid to be "different," of appearing excited over things that one was not supposed to become excited about. After all, dissent did not become popular on the campus until *after* it had been widely discussed, proved and analyzed by the media and sociologists, and courted by some politicians; until, in fact, it became a form of conformism. In 1953-54, on the contrary, movies about the feats of the F.B.I. were as frequent and popular as more recently those about the revolt of the young. Newspapers, magazines, television were "selling" the iniquities of Communism and virtues of the American way of life as strenuously as they have during the last three or four years the "generation gap," and the evils of alienated industrialized society. And, of course, the Korean conflict had been concluded after only three years, as against the long-festering sore of Vietnam.

The defense of academic freedom from the frontal attack of McCarthyism and from its lingering echoes in the form of loyalty oaths, was thus confined largely to the faculties as well as (occasionally) boards of trustees. As I have suggested above, some psychological wounds were never healed, but it would be a gross misstatement to say that when the smoke of the battle cleared in the mid-1950s, the American university

was less free, its teachers or students more afraid to speak up
their minds than had been the case five or six years before.

THE AMERICAN UNIVERSITY apparently resumed its
placid and prosperous existence. Like the rest of society, it
became engrossed with growth: more buildings, more
students, more faculty, more administrators.

That in general this growth was inevitable, that much of it
was beneficial, there can be no doubt. Yet there were certain
aspects of it which should have been disquieting, and which
were to prove unfortunate. One of the great strengths of
American higher education had been its diversity, and it is
difficult to find a more appropriate word. There were very
good large universities as well as small colleges, residential
schools as well as those in the large cities which offered
opportunities to a student who had to or preferred to live at
home; colleges which purported to be austerely intellectual,
as well as those which acknowledged freely, sometimes too
freely, that education need not be a terribly earnest and
strenuous affair; some which were religious in their emphasis,
others unabashedly secular. In all of them there was much
room for improvement, but there was absolutely no need to
strive for uniformity. Why should Columbia, Amherst, and
Notre Dame all try to be similar—rather than improve
instruction, increase salaries, etc., and still cultivate their
interesting differences and peculiarities?

Yet this is what was happening in the 1950s. Harvard was
rather awkwardly trying to introduce religiosity while Notre
Dame, even in those pre-ecumenical days, was becoming
visibly embarrassed by its emphasis on religion. And every
institution had to grow! One would have thought that in a
country as vast and as rich there was plenty of room for new
universities and centers of learning. The universities' unin-
hibited growth was already affecting unfavorably some
communities. The turbulence of the next decade could not

be foreseen, but what could be forecast was that piling up students and buildings into the limited space of a Berkeley, Cambridge, or Boston was bound to create serious problems for the universities and communities concerned. This growth, in turn, enhanced the importance and influence of the educational bureaucracy which was to become a nation-wide class with ramifications in the government, foundations, as well as schools themselves, with its natural tendency to think of education in quantitative terms, federal funds, national goals and the like, and with its almost inevitable, even if usually unintended, disparagement of the point of view of the scholar, with his "narrow specialization" and his incomprehensible peculiarities and interests. The old-fashioned dean firmly moored to one institution was already being replaced by a brisk administrator now at *X* college, then at *Y* university, then perhaps in a foundation or a government agency, equipped with statistics and attuned to national issues and urgencies rather than parochial interests of the given school. It was already foreseeable that interest in education would grow to the point where the atmosphere might become incompatible with scholarship and learning, and that solicitude for students *en masse* would make it hard for the university to provide a proper setting for the development of the individual. Bureaucratic mentality tends to be overly serious, and the air of grim purposefulness does not go well with education. Even before they were to be told that they were to save the world, the students were already being pestered and indoctrinated about "achievement," a variety of "challenges," and how we were witnessing the race between education and disaster. No wonder that the latter was to catch up, and that many students were to cry out against this strange ethos which, rather than diminishing the natural anxieties of the young, has tended to maximize them.

The appearance and growth of the class of academic

administrators would not have been so significant without certain parallel developments within the academic profession itself. The postwar period brought not only prosperity, but also what might be described as a redistribution of importance and national attention among various branches of learning. Seemingly, the greatest gains in these respects were scored by sciences. Those previously most academic of academic pursuits—mathematics and theoretical physics—became endowed with vast national and practical importance. To be sure, there were grave disadvantages to this new situation. Who in the 1920s would have thought that political views and youthful associations of a physicist could become the object of nation-wide attention and political dispute? By the same token, how many scientists would have assumed before the Second World War that because of their professional expertise, their views on foreign policy and domestic politics carried a greater weight or deserved more consideration than those of an average citizen? Apart from the prying activities of congressional committees the problem was still real. A general in active service was supposed to eschew political affiliations and public statements. Was Professor X who advised the government on nuclear weapons less involved in the nation's security hence to be freer from a scrutiny of his past and views and from requirements of discretion than a general? Even in the 1950s one could foresee the making of a future conflict. On the one hand, you had a lingering suspicion in the public mind (and at times as during the McCarthy controversy, more than just that) of the academic establishment; while within the academic community you had a parallel suspicion of the government plus at least a tinge of certain elitist feelings. Of course, professors had the right to advise on matters of national importance and the government a duty to listen to them, but this did not mean that they should be subjected to demeaning regulations and restrictions binding on public servants. You had the phenomenon, partly disheartening, partly comical, of various government security agencies questioning one about political views and peculiarities of one's colleagues and students.

The problem could not have been avoided yet it could have, with a degree of prudence and foresight on both sides, been minimized. The universities could have insisted that the bulk of scientific work for the government, whether classified or not, should be done directly under its sponsorship and in special organizations distinct from academic institutions; the U.S. government could have done much more than it has in developing a sort of scientific civil service. The government, or if one prefers to put it this way, the country has and will continue to need the services of professors and experts, but it is not conducive to an academic atmosphere to have the university as a place where you have frequent security checks, massive classified research, and the personnel divided into those who have been "cleared" for secret work and those who have not.

But the eventual harm of the failure to think this problem through was to go much deeper. It was naive to hope that the university could become enmeshed with the government, aspire to *political* influence and yet escape becoming involved with politics. And it was not even in sciences that this involvement was to become most far-reaching and damaging, but in the social sciences.

The traditional role of the social scientist has been that of an observer, analyst, and critic. As such, at times he has, of course, exercised enormous influence on public attitudes and policies. But this influence, traditionally and properly, has been indirect. Lord Keynes' theories transformed postwar economic and fiscal policies of Britain and the United States, but these policies had first to be legislated by Parliament and Congress and then put into effect by the appropriate government agencies. The theory of democracy does not admit the existence of a class which has a monopoly on political wisdom, and a unique insight into social problems. It draws a sharp distinction between the role of the expert and that of the policy-maker, between intellectual influence on policy making and political power. Thus, *if we believe in democracy,* it may be deplorable but it is still right that the views of the majority should prevail even against a unanimous judgment of experts in the given field. An enlightened government will give special weight to the opinion of an expert, a civilized community will accord a respectful hearing to the views of a distinguished intellectual even in a field in which he is not an expert. But the road to political *power* has to lead through the ballot box. Thus when Woodrow Wilson, then a leading political scientist and educator, sought political power, he did so as an office-seeker by running first for governor and then for president.

This very obvious, in fact commonplace, distinction became gradually blurred. Even in the 1950s the idea began to gain ground that intellectuals or professors constituted a special constituency or pressure group. At first this was harmless. Many of the species grew unusually ready, nay eager, to append their signatures to political endorsements and statements on public issues where even they professed no special competence. But, after all, the same practice caught on in the world of sports and entertainment. And initially at least, support by the "eggheads" (what, by the way, has happened to this term?) was thought to be more of a political liability rather than an asset. Dwight Eisenhower enjoyed more support among football coaches while Adlai Stevenson topped him among professors; and Eisenhower won. But already in 1956 managers of the Republican campaign went to some pains to publicize the fact that some prominent eggheads were supporting their candidate.

It would be inaccurate and unjust to accuse the academic profession of being thirsty for power, or to say that a majority or even a significant minority of its members began to think of themselves as an elite whose views on politics and society should be unquestioningly heeded by the vulgar politicians. Greater participation by academic personnel, especially social scientists, in policy formulation and execution at all levels of government was a natural consequence of the evolution of politics and policies since the war. The development of the welfare state, vast programs of foreign aid and of help with social and economic development abroad: all those programs and tasks called for specially qualified people, and they were to be found largely in the universities. The influx of academics into government services could no more be faulted or considered sinister than that of lawyers or businessmen.

But the trouble has been not with academic people being involved with Washington, but with academic *institutions* becoming involved with policies and politics. And even more fundamentally and regrettably, the general political configuration was beginning to affect the nature of academic pursuit, especially in the social sciences.

This is not the place to discuss the vexing question of how "scientific" the social sciences can or ought to become. But there is no question that the worldly as well as intellectual success of science has had not an altogether favorable influence on the morale and motivations of the social scientists. Mathematics and physics were (to use this term before it acquired the present unfortunate connotations) relevant, mathematicians and physicists were important. They did not merely describe various theories and formulate their own; they stated and discovered truths about the universe which could not be understood or contested by a politician, but which often had a direct bearing on the policy of the United States government. How irrelevant, especially to himself and in secret, must have appeared many a social scientist who in 1960 as in 1900 still talked about Aristotle, about the background and motivations of the founders of the

U.S. Constitution, about theories of value, and the like, whose conclusions could not be clothed in the air of inconvertibility but had to be tentative, whose discoveries could not help or threaten the defense or welfare of the United States. Perhaps only the economists could, as a body, escape this galling if often unconscious feeling of inferiority vis-à-vis their scientific colleagues; *their* findings after all could also have momentous importance. But even they could not match that infuriating certainty which to a *non-scientist* seems to characterize the nature of scientific discovery. A physicist may be a Communist or a rock-ribbed Republican, yet this does not affect his view of the quantum theory. But how often have equally distinguished economists found themselves clashing on some fundamental theoretical or policy problem?

To these gloomy reflections by a sociologist or political scientist—for all the world cared, or was likely to feel the difference, he might as well work on Shakespeare or ancient Greek pottery—were often added considerations of a more crass nature. Scientists were basking in federal funds, in celebrity or notoriety, advised in the Pentagon or were pursued by a congressional committee. To be sure, federal and private largesse was already flowing into social science research; an expert on Russia, China, or economic development was likely to command some attention, be listened to, or investigated. But it was not quite the same thing. And besides where did it leave the bulk of social scientists?

Let me hasten to add that such considerations (and, in fact, being very human they cannot be deemed in any way to be discreditable) were far from universal within the honorable and eminently useful professions of history, economics, sociology, and political science. But whatever the psychological mechanism behind it, there was the undeniable tendency for their practitioners to assert themselves, to try to become more scientific in the strict sense of the word, and to become more important in the eyes of society.

The social scientist began to reach for and employ the language and tools of science. Venerable professors of political science and sociology who had forgotten their high school mathematics now plunged into calculus, probed the mysteries of the number theory, required their assistants to work with computers. This transformation became known as "re-tooling." It became quite fashionable, whether the subject under discussion was the Supreme Court decisions or Communist ideology, for articles in professional journals to have at least a few equations and graphs. The new wave became known as behaviorism. In fact, the term social sciences has tended to become replaced by the more "scientific" sounding "behavioral sciences." Measurement became the goal and the highest good of behaviorism; "value judgments," that alleged and infamous vice of old-fashioned social science, the main enemy.

At their best, the new techniques had something to recommend them and their practitioners something to offer. There was need and room for greater precision and for a wider use of statistical and mathematical methods in dealing with social and political problems of the present and past. Yet by the same token the new approach, when pursued in an uncritical spirit, was bound to become a mere ritual or worse a form of obscurantism masquerading as science. Elaborate graphs, equations, esoteric vocabulary, would often be employed only to end up with platitudinous conclusions. New terms and categories should not be introduced until absolutely necessary, according to a famous philosophical maxim. Shaved by this Occam's razor, many a monograph in sociology or political science would entirely disappear. There was a disquieting note of intolerance about this new enthusiasm, many of the zealots proclaiming that humanistic and esthetic considerations and historical antecedents were excess baggage and had no place in the science of society.*

In academic pursuits, as in everything else, the eventual advance is often a by-product of previous over-emphasis and exaggeration of the benefits of the new approach or theory. But what made the new fashion in the social sciences so disturbing was the rapidity with which it spread through institutions of higher learning. It is as if a bell had rung sometime in the middle '50s and suddenly universities, foundations, and the relevant government institutions began to "shape up" according to the new dispensation. Recently, of course, we have become quite accustomed to this phenomenon, as evidenced in the mushroom growth of New Economics, New Politics, etc. But at the time, and though the new wave had no apparent political underprinnings, one had already cause to reflect how *easily* untested novelty could find general acceptance in the universities' curricula, and how rapidly unreflecting zeal could gain a foothold within the academic community. The major universities had performed creditably in defending academic freedom, but now one had to wonder whether they could do equally well in defending academic and rational standards against intellectual fads and fashions often bordering on obscurantism.

In addition to becoming quasi-scientific, social studies were becoming (as the phrase went and still goes) "policy oriented." This too, in itself, was to a large extent inevitable and beneficial. Government was becoming more important in

---

*In true American style the pendulum was to swing very rapidly and to the other unreasonable extreme. In recent professional convocations, inspired allegedly by the New Left, partisans of Motivation and Positive Social Action have grappled with the devotees of Measurement and Value-Free social science. The former assert that the latter, while pretending to be objective scientists, are in fact apologists and defenders of the iniquitous *status quo*. One feels that the new radicals give their opponents too much credit: sometimes it is just impossible to decipher what *they* say or want.

American life, more and more social problems were assumed to be susceptible to political solution. A sociologist teaching a course on crime and delinquency could not be expected *not* to indicate what legal reforms might be beneficial, what in his view were social and economic remedies which also might bring desirable results. Ditto concerning a lawyer or political scientist teaching a course on civil rights, or an economist instructing in collective bargaining. Nor could one realistically have expected that in his discussion of issues of political importance the teacher could be entirely unbiased, or uncontroversial. A scrupulous teacher might, of course, indicate his biases or where he *thought* his objectivity ended and speculation on politics began. But, unlike what many believe, bias or even real or alleged indoctrination have *not* been the main danger arising out of this great growth of courses dealing with problems of current political and social importance.

The principal danger has been the mere growth in the number of such courses, and the weight they have assumed in the curriculum of an average college student. First, this tended to create the illusion, and a dangerous one it was to prove, that the university is the main place where social and political problems are discussed and where solutions for them are or ought to be devised. Again, this clashes directly with one of the main premises of democracy, as well as with those of liberal education. No one has delegated to the American university, to its faculty or students, the right to devise solutions or to pronounce authoritative dicta on what *should* be our policy toward China, on the race issue or on anything else. On political and social issues of current importance all the university can and should do is to produce knowledge: *i.e.,* men who will advance knowledgeable and hopefully persuasive arguments to the *national* discussion of such issues. But beginning with the period under discussion it has been drawn to try to do more. Its professors have tended not only to teach and study but also to prescribe; to assume, and to act accordingly, that they had not only information but definitive answers.

It has been a heartening, but as yet unproved tenet of the American educational creed that by expending a lot of effort on the given social and political problem, *i.e.*, through massive study, research and money, one best advances desirable solutions. But it is at least debatable whether the best way for a student to acquire a balanced outlook on current social and political problems is to be immersed in them to the point of neglecting other facets of formal education. The British for some time have operated a most successful civil service on the assumption that the best way to prepare a young man to administer a district in India, or to consider alternative schemes of taxation, was to put him through a largely classical or scientific education. Do many courses on current (and to be sure, important) issues contain much over and above what an attentive reader of better newspapers and magazines can gather for himself? Are all the insights about American foreign policy or urban problems to be gathered in a course about American foreign policy or urban problems, or can one get a more valuable perspective from a course in history or psychology? The whole advance of science, indeed most of the progress in civilization, has been premised, in fact, on the rejection of the crude notion that the only yardstick in measuring the value of a given branch of knowledge was its *immediate* usefulness. Yet even in those quiet and prosperous days universities, *i.e.*, their administrators and many faculty members, were not wise and far-seeing enough to resist the temptation to immerse themselves in policy problems and contentions.

In the absence of strong insitutional resistance and self-restraint the temptation grew almost irresistible. Who in 1930 would have thought that the proper place for working out military strategies was not the general staff but a university seminar, that formulation of economic priorities for the nation was the task of professors rather than congressmen? Yet by 1960 almost everybody had agreed that the university was a proper place for those pursuits. The notion that academic study of politics, or of social and military problems, gains favor and is primarily useful insofar as it is done in *detachment* from day to day involvement with such problems had become discredited. On the contrary, a professor's reputation was often enhanced and his promotion more rapid if he moved in the proximity of power and politics. Even a graduate student might now envisage his future accomplishments not in terms of scholarly mono-graphs and intellectual influence but as a future policy-maker and adviser to presidential candidates. In choosing the life of the mind one did not any more, it was felt, forsake the exciting world of affairs. In fact, the shortcut to the corridors of power might lead through the seminar room.

The number of actual statesmen-professors was still quite small, but their example and influence already far-reaching. If Professor X was advising the government and basking in the status of national celebrity on this count, there was some incentive for his colleague Y to offer his though as yet unsolicited reflections on this or that national policy, perhaps to shape his research and work so that they would bear on affairs of national importance and attention. Again, this eagerness of so many academicians to foresake the quiet of their study or laboratory and to volunteer their services to the republic was quite natural and, in some cases, laudable. But what was already striking and unhealthy was the growing disposition of the academic community (and the seeming acceptance of that by society) to consider the university not only as the repository of specialized knowledge and expertise but also of wisdom. The stereotype of that kindly unworldly professor of not so long ago was being displaced by one of a stern arbiter of what should be national policy on arms limitation, foreign aid, or social welfare.

IT WOULD BE RIDICULOUS of course, to claim that the academic profession in 1960 thought of itself or was in the process of becoming a ruling class in America or that it was even close to wielding power and influence comparable to that of the business community before the Great Depression. Yet the extent and character of its involvement with things non-academic helped to weaken and confuse the university's proper function. In another decade American universities would be confronted with absurd and outrageous demands which, however, largely because of their previous sins of commission, their administrations would find hard to resist. The universities, the radicals would claim, had helped to formulate and provide personnel for the execution of the U.S. imperialist policies abroad and for perpetuation of capitalist exploitation at home, Wasn't it, then, at least fair that they should offer opportunities for instruction and for teachers who would unmask that imperialism, and spell out ways by which participatory democracy might replace the present iniquitous system. Here is a professor who has advised on some U.S. policies in Vietnam; how can the university then bar a man from teaching on the grounds that he has advocated the violent overthrow of the government? Even the so-called moderates would advance claims which a few years before a radical would have deemed preposterous and impractical. Here is this rich institution with all its resourceful people, committed to social progress—why, then, has it not solved *all* the major social and economic problems of the city in which it is located? At the time when the academic institutions were already in the throes of a serious crisis and unable to perform their proper functions, it was to be seriously proposed that they should venture into all sorts of extraneous enterprises. At one time, I believe in 1968-69, it was seriously proposed that the Harvard School of Education, then experiencing troubles with its own students, should assume the responsibility for the administration of a particularly troublesome public school district in *New York*. But had not universities in the past devised economic plans for foreign countries?

The vast expansion of the university, the excessive proliferation of activities for which it was not really suited, the assumption that it was capable not only of analyzing and instructing but of advising and prescribing, the burgeoning of pseudo-science and of intra-university bureaucracy—all those interlocking phenomena which were amply observable in the late 1950s would have undoubtedly led to a serious crisis of higher education even without Vietnam. In addition there was another reason if not for apprehension then for the proverbial somber reflection, but here the universities merely reflected a general tendency in American culture of the period. I refer to the role that Dr. Freud and various offshoots of the teachings and philosophy of the Vienna sage were assuming in American life.

Here I might digress and assert somewhat dogmatically that the business of running a school or indeed a society becomes virtually impossible unless we assume that *most* people do things they do because they want to. The problem of their deeper psychological motivations is an interesting and important one; it provides employment for psychologists and psychoanalysts, material for better novelists, etc. But how do you fix responsibility for any individual act, or decide the validity of any personal preference in the absence of that perhaps vulgar but necessary maxim? It is especially necessary for a democracy, for without it the democratic process loses any meaning. You have fifty-one per cent of the people voting for a given candidate, and that is that, according to the unsophisticated criteria of the bygone age.

"Ah, but," a sophisticated critic would object, "did they *really* vote for Mr. *X* or were they acting out various anxieties and complexes only superficially linked to the given name or party? What were they *really* trying to say?" Can political authority based on such a casual expression of various fears and hang-ups be really legitimate? What, then, is a political or historical fact? Most non-Communists would readily agree that between 1944 and 1948 Soviet Russia, often using atrocious means, subjugated various East European countries. But aren't facts greatly misleading, to the point practically when they cease to be facts (or so would some devotees of the deeper cause school agree)? Wasn't Stalin acting out of a severe feeling of insecurity? Isn't it a *fact* that there was great hostility toward Russia and Communism in *this* country? When student disorders first hit the American campuses, one would have thought that the starting point of any discussion of causes and remedies would have been the indisputable fact that some *individuals,* most of whom were students, seized some buildings and violated some other regulations and conventions. But no, the discussion both within the university and in the country at large immediately shifted to that philosophical question—were "the Students," *i.e.,* presumably the eight or so million of them, rightly alienated from society, or were they, on the contrary, products of an over-permissive society? Sophisticated opinion would have greeted with incredulity, pity, and contempt the simple assertion that whether the students were alienated or their behavior was the product of over-permissiveness was, indeed, an interesting question and one which just *might* be resolved through discussion and dialogues, but that it had little or no direct connection with some individual persons seizing buildings, or with the problem of preventing such occurrences in the future.

But even apart from such drama (and when such violence was still unforeseen and unimaginable), it was clear that the teaching of Freud and of his followers—so profound and useful, so enlightening in many cases or analyses of the springs of human motivation—was being turned into a cult and as such was saturating American educational institutions. Within the universities this proliferation of psychological analysis and interest was accomplishing in one respect what the excessive expansion of policy "how to do it" courses was doing at another: deflecting higher learning from its proper focus, feeding the dangerous illusion that its main purpose was *immediate* application to social and personal problems. An undergraduate might feel after emerging from a series of sociology and political science courses that he now qualified as a social reformer and knew social truths inaccessible to the vulgar multitude. And from an array of courses on personality, small group psychology, and the like, he would often derive equally superficial sophistication about the springs of human behavior. It is one of the traditional clichés about higher education that one of its aims is to make the student challenge traditional beliefs and values. But, in effect, what the student would get in exchange for the old beliefs would be what by now has achieved the status of a traditional jargon. Not infrequently he would confuse boredom and resentment with "alienation" and would be too ready to identify that irresolution and uncertainty about one's direction, so typical of a certain stage of growth, with the "identity crisis." His mind would not become freer nor his critical capacity enriched but rather the place of old dogmas and beliefs would be taken by indoctrination with a mishmash of ritualistic phrases, clichés, and pseudo-scientific concepts.

To say that is not to denigrate the role of psychological and sociological study nor the illumination they have provided to other social sciences. It is simply to observe the undue weight they have assumed in the college curricula and unjustified pretensions to scientific exactitude *some* of their practitioners have advanced. Even a lover of ancient culture will not claim today that classics should still constitute the core of higher education or that an authority on Greek or Latin must be an infallible arbiter of esthetic and humanistic values. But the devotees of psychological and psychoanalytical techniques have in many cases been like those followers of a new and militant nationalism: intolerant and contemptuous of others' points of view, filled with a holy zeal, convinced that the whole world was theirs to conquer or at least to analyze.

Instead of serving only as an occasional seasoning, the new approach (or, if one prefers, faith) became an important ingredient of the educational fare. Here the author, though unlicensed, must risk a psychologico-educational observation of his own: young people, even without any prompting, are given to considerable brooding over their own psyche, their inadequacy of one sort or another. Is it wise to encourage this concern and to elevate it into an academic discipline? The traditional educational approach always insisted on the importance of drawing people outside themselves, always took the stand that education could help with personal as well as social problems—but *not directly.* Yet the American university was already attuned to problem solving: it was in the classroom and the seminar that one was seeking and supposedly finding answers not only to what should be U.S. foreign policy or the rate of economic growth in Pakistan, but also concerning one's personality development and psychological well-being. Was it, then, inconceivable that those two aspects of the university as the school of life might become mixed up, that the teachers might suggest and students might believe that most of one's personal problems were the fault of society, or even that political or social activism be used as a kind of group therapy?

At the time (which is, to repeat, around 1960), few as yet thought of establishing that connection. There were, to be sure, a few philosophers instructing on the evils of industrialized society, on how it violates and represses the individual by compelling him to abide by materialistic standards, etc. But this theme, in itself a very old one, was not as yet widely heeded nor was it thought to have any connection with rock music or the length of one's hair; Elvis Presley's (the Beatles were as yet unknown) and Dr. Herbert Marcuse's constituencies were still quite distinct, and the latter's was still very small. The cult of primitivism was quite a few years away. Those mass gatherings of the young, so much applauded for their primitive innocence and small incidence of violence, were still inconceivable. (Indeed if one reflects on the life of an aboriginal society it is, except insofar as its members have to earn their living, one continuous Woodstock festival.) The university, in other words, still had not become the focus and symbol of various cults as well as political dissent and social disturbance.

Who could have told that those changes in college curricula, the growing emphasis on policy and personality studies, the increase in the number of social scientists, were warning signs as well as contributory causes to what was to be America's cultural revolution? As yet only academic pedants and purists would protest that some of their colleagues were too much interested in the exciting world of affairs in Washington, or in stimulating the young to be execssively interested in themselves.

After all, is there a firm line between academic and utilitarian concerns? The Harvard Business School had been for long an accepted part of the academic establishment, and few could deny that it has made important contributions not only in teaching managerial skills, but in such fields of research as industrial psychology. Its claim to imparting worldly wisdom through academic techniques was rather far-reaching; its faculty contained not only professors of management, finance and merchandising but also, as their title specifically stated, of human relations. It was, therefore, not too surprising, nor seemingly alarming, that other departments of the university should seek to dispense practical wisdom as well as learning. One midwestern university actually has on its faculty a professor of decision making!

In all seriousness, conditions of modern life made it almost impossible to separate neatly academic from practical and social concerns. The academic community would have been denounced, and probably justly so, if it had tried to stay away and not lend its skills to solutions of the latter. And the average professor or expert could not always be expected to keep his academic and public personalities separate. Archimedes served—as a combination of Henry Kissinger and Edward Teller—the government of ancient Syracuse. And yet as Plutarch tells us,

> . . . repudiating as sordid and ignoble the whole trade of engineering and every sort of art that lends itself to mere use and profit, he placed his whole affection and ambition in those purer speculations where there can be no reference to the vulgar needs of life; studies the superiority of which to all others is unquestioned and in which the only doubt can be whether the beauty and grandeur of the subjects explored, or the precision and cogency of the methods and means of proof, most deserve our admiration.*

A modern Archimedes could not duplicate such heroic devotion and self-restraint. For one, he would be accused of lacking social conscience.

Still, can even a modern university prosper unless it places as its ideal and focus of its activities "those purer speculations"? By trying to be *excessively* practical, of immediate help to its students and to society at large, the

---

*Plutarch, *The Lives of the Noble Grecians and Romans,* translated by John Dryden (New York: Modern Library, 1940), p. 378.

university was not only becoming vulnerable to future criticism that it is taking sides on social and political issues, (that it is not doing "enough") but also impairing that vast and beneficial, even if indirect, influence on society and its students that a properly functioning university has always exercised. One can confidently assert that had the trend of the late 1950s continued, even without a massive U.S. involvement in Southeast Asia, the American university would have become crippled. Its decline would have been less rapid and dramatic and perhaps less tied to political passions. But there would have still been alienation: *i.e.,* a sizeable proportion of students becoming restless and bored. There would still have been a continuous dilution of the scholarly interest of its faculty: *i.e.,* a growing number of university administrators and teachers fancying themselves as policy-makers and social engineers rather than educators.

ONE MIGHT ASK *who* was guilty, and *why* those trends were not resisted more vigorously. There were in small as well as large universities teachers and administrators devoted to scholarly values and deeply disturbed by the new tendencies in higher education as well as within their own institutions. But there were reasons why their warnings were not heeded and their opposition usually ineffective.

In the first place, there was prosperity. This often dulls the sense of danger and makes people unduly tolerant. If it was proposed to set up a new field of study or institute of dubious relationship to the purposes of higher learning, it could still be and was usually argued that the essential functions of the school would not suffer: there was plenty of money to go around. Why should one begrudge an academic connection for an Institute of Current Affairs, or a school of journalism, or a title of professor for the practitioners of those arts? Wasn't one being stuffy, or snobbish, or both? The same went for the great increase in the number of college administrators. The country was growing richer, people of college age were having more problems, and hence needed more attention. You need not worry that that new dean would mean one less professor of Greek! The same psychology led to relaxed vigilance, "lowering the standards," as the phrase went. Why not appoint X who dabbles in some currently fashionable (but, as yet, suspect in the eyes of the more conservative members of his profession) techniques? The "innovator" would not be blocking the path for a man whose scholarly credentials were above suspicion.

Academic like all other criteria are fallible. People who are to pass on them even (or perhaps especially) at the leading institutions are often smug about their own credentials and less than charitable about those of others. "What has *he* published recently?" would say disdainfully Professor X to his colleague Y, both of rather mediocre accomplishment, in reference to a man who had made a fundamental contribution to his discipline ten or fifteen years before. And, in contrast, the man of great scholarly fertility would often be suspect for writing too much, for being almost (horrible to say) a popularizer. For all such human failings, standards for appointing people to permanent academic positions in the respectable institutions had risen impressively in the postwar years. It became *almost* inconceivable that the preference of a donor—or political consideration of any sort—might determine the incumbent of a university position. But now this vigilance and zeal visibly slackened.

Another reason, apart from but obviously connected with prosperity, was the *apparently* flourishing condition of the university. There was undeniable evidence as well as solid substance of progress: students were better prepared; the American high school had improved and had not as yet become a battleground of conflicting educational ideologies. The teachers were better paid. There could be no doubt that the level of instruction had risen, and so had that of the scholarly attainment of the faculty of the average as well as leading colleges. The disquieting phenomena of which we spoke could be rationalized as a temporary ailment rather than an ascending trend. Optimism is deeply ingrained in the American nature; it is practically a tenet of the secular faith. And so after the McCarthy era, the universities were pleased with the disappearance of their tormentors, and pleased with their growth and with the new and unusual deference society was beginning to pay them.

And here was another reason why the university was set, as the 1960s began, on its dangerous course. After first paying scant attention to it, then regarding it with considerable suspicion, American society, suddenly it seemed, began to regard its universities as repositories of practical as well as theoretical wisdom, the laboratories where the most pressing social problems *ought* to be studied, and solutions worked out. The change was dazzling in its apparent rapidity. Here a few years before, universities were often regarded as nests of subversion, their professors dragged before congressional committees, forced to confess their ancient sins and promise repentance, their presidents tearfully pleading with their trustees or legislatives. Now the professors would still go to Washington but this time to lay down the law to generals and admirals, to explain the economic imperatives to government agencies dispensing economic aid abroad, and sociological and psychological guide lines to the bureaucrats promoting domestic reforms. The president of a major university would no longer be a supplicant for understanding and funds. In a few years his image grew into that of a masterful administrator, a man automatically qualified for any Cabinet post, whose opinions on matters of national and international importance would be sought as eagerly as those of a major industrialist.

Society itself had grown extremely (some might say: excessively and unhealthily) interested in what was going on in institutions of higher education, and not only on Saturday afternoons in the fall. This interest had accumulated since the development of nuclear energy and received an additional impetus in the wake of the Soviets putting into orbit their first satellite. But not only mathematicians and physicists were now of obvious and frightening importance. The social scientists also had some important works to sell—how to avoid inflation, how to organize foreign policy, etc. And you had the college administrators who, since they managed (as it was believed) all those important people with their mysterious skills, were themselves qualified for the highest positions. The national press and magazines began to refer to university presidents and deans in terms hitherto reserved for high business executives and military and naval figures: "dynamic," "high powered," "tough minded," "soft spoken." The universities were expected to be in the news; their administrators and even some faculty grew accustomed to, and were expected to make pronouncements of national importance and interest. These expectations were to be more than fulfilled in the decade which lay ahead.

3

The
Temptations of Academe

JOHN F. KENNEDY liked professors and academic surroundings. Why it should have been so still awaits answers from a future historian, for with all due deference to Mr. Arthur M. Schlesinger who holds the opposite view, we do need a longer perspective on certain historical events and problems. In the meantime one can only speculate. Did the young politician find in an academic environment a welcome distraction from his Washington routine? Was it for him a relief from the somewhat oppressive expectations placed on him by his family, from his role as the representative of Catholicism and Irishness in the higher echelons of what would soon be called the Establishment? Whatever the reasons, he was often around his university, more than would be warranted in the case of an average dutiful alumnus who was also a young and busy man. He evidently relished his appearances in a seminar on American politics. Elected an overseer of Harvard in the late 1950s, he chose to serve out his term after becoming president. In contemplating what he would do after leaving the high office at a relatively early age, he apparently thought seriously of becoming a professor. Kennedy gave every evidence of liking what was then the style of academic life, or at least what it must have appeared to be to somebody quite close to but not within the academic world. In his discussions with students and professors he gave every impression of being at ease, with no hint of that certain stiffness and nervousness marking his political appearances.

Professors, for their part, took some time to warm up to the then senator from Massachusetts. He was Joseph Kennedy's son, and the former ambassador's pre-Pearl Harbor isolationist views and his friendship with Joseph McCarthy were still remembered. He was a practicing Catholic, again in the eyes of practicing liberals not an asset in those pre-ecumenical days. Kennedy's views while in Congress could hardly be described as those of the advanced liberal variety. But eventually the senator's charm, quick intelligence and rising political fortunes prevailed over such shortcomings. In liberal intellectual circles there was considerable nostalgia for Adlai Stevenson, but by 1960 it was clear he was going nowhere. Hubert Humphrey, once second in the hearts of that group, had little of his rival's youthful charm and suddenly, though he was a licensed political scientist, he appeared almost non-intellectual when compared with Kennedy. As to the election itself, there would be no question where the loyalty of a vast majority of liberal professors would lie; Mr. Nixon was no more popular among them then than he is now.

The full extent of John F. Kennedy's assimilation into the liberal academe became evident only after the election. It became clear that he not only used but leaned on professors. Quantitatively, the new administration marked the culmination of a trend rather than a drastic new departure: ever since at least 1933, and for obvious reasons, the successive

Washington regimes increasingly employed people of academic background. Now, however, it was not merely a question of numbers. The spirit of the new team was definitely academic. The young president himself, often frustrated by domestic and baffled by foreign politicians, would find relief and understanding in the *congerie* of his advisers who came from the university rather than the business or political worlds.

The academic flavor of the new administration was to weigh heavily on its policies, both domestic and foreign. Yet, to anticipate some of the future discussion, it would be unfair and incorrect to describe it as being *dominated* by a handful of intellectuals from a few Eastern universities. Mr. Kennedy was sufficiently close to that world to know its inherent limitations. It was his successor who let himself be unduly impressed by the academic notables he had inherited. Here, then, was the all-too-frequent paradox, a man who views himself and is regarded by others as a hard-boiled man of affairs deferring to those who come from the world of ideas, who talk and write well and, sometimes, glibly.

I do not propose here to play the game "what-would-have-happened-if." Nor is it just or reasonable to blame all the troubles which have descended on our heads on "liberal intellectuals" or "professors." In our thinking about great historical events we (*i.e.,* the Americans) oscillate too much between extremes: we see either a plot or grim historical forces before which human ingenuity and intelligence stand helpless. It was *not* the House of Morgan which brought about the Great Depression, it was *not* a handful of Harvard professors "who got us into Vietnam." But on the other hand, things don't "just happen." Human error rather than moral wickedness is responsible for many historical catastrophes, but this error proceeds most often from excessive self-confidence or what in the language of theology is classified as pride (which, incidentally, *is* a moral failing). Alas, this quality is not uncommon among professors in our leading institutions.

Those who went to Washington when the decade opened brought with them a strong conviction that they were smarter, more liberal, more "with it" than the dull crew of Republican businessmen who had preceded them. They were probably right on all those counts, and yet ... Brilliance is not always accompanied by common sense; solicitude for the poor and down-trodden not always a guarantee that those who are inspired by it will do things which benefit those groups. Elegance and the enjoyment of power (or of being near it) may become, if too self-conscious, rather tawdry. It is not unfair to suggest that many of the newcomers felt that things at home and abroad should become immediately better because now there were such brilliant, and interesting people to deal with them. When this, in many respects, did not happen, the professorial New Frontiersmen would grow confused, attribute reasons for such perplexing adversities to the incomprehension and obsolete thinking of the professionals: the military with their antediluvian notions, the diplomats with their anti-democratic biases and their pedantic objections to ingenious new initiatives. It took some time for the newcomers to realize how intractable some problems, especially in the foreign field, were; or at least how they failed to respond to even the most liberal slogans, or to the most original position papers. Khrushchev was unmoved by the new administration's friendly overtures and its open mind on social and political change throughout the world. De Gaulle might be impressed how well Mrs. Kennedy and the president's assistant spoke French, but he still dourly set himself against some of America's principal policies and goals. Leaders of the Third World were enthusiastic about the new president's personality, but a Ben Bella or Sukarno would still seek political inspiration in Moscow or Peking.

There was obvious bewilderment among members of the new administration, why the undoubted good will and intelligence in its policies were not yielding immediate and tangible benefits. In foreign policy the disillusionment was sharpest: the lamentable circumstances attending the Bay of Pigs episode and the incredible bullying to which the president was submitted by Khrushchev during their Vienna meeting produced that confusion and loss of self-confidence in the U.S. foreign policy from which it was to emerge (but not entirely) after the Cuban missile crisis. One is tempted to lay down some conclusions about the influence of academics and about the consequent distinction of the style of the new regime from the preceding one. If the Eisenhower-Dulles line was too rigid and insensitive, simply holding the fort against "Godless Communism," then the new people were too sensitive, too eager to be innovative. The administration was almost *too* responsive to criticism and suggestions: what some Oxford intellectuals and some newspapermen in Saigon said and felt was allowed to assume great importance.

IN THE DOMESTIC FIELD the impact of what might be called the academic mind was more varied and subtle. One cannot refrain from observing that it was most beneficial in the one field where the people whose advice was followed were not merely talented and liberal but also had a profound knowledge of their subject, namely economics. When it came to broader social and political issues, the administration was unduly prone to believe that brilliant people will unfailingly come up with brilliant solutions, even when it comes to exceedingly complex and delicate issues. Mr. Schlesinger mentions in his account of the Kennedy era how when it came to forming the Cabinet two names would repeatedly turn up as those of men qualified to occupy any high position. They were two university presidents whose schools were to be most seriously affected during the student troubles of the coming decade and who then felt constrained to leave their posts. It is not suggested that the gentlemen concerned were directly responsible for their universities finding themselves in the eye of the storm. But the story may serve as an illustration of how strongly it was felt *c.* 1961-62 that a university administrator was *ex-officio* more enlightened, more capable of dealing with serious domestic problems than a mere politician or a business executive. The academic bureaucrat as well as the professor found himself transferred often to a post in the government. It is perhaps not extravagant to state that, in the 1960s, to the already flourishing military-industrial complex was joined the not inconsiderable academic-bureaucratic one.

The permeation of Washington by this academic atmosphere was undoubtedly responsible for the special accent on youth so pronounced in public statements and policies. Here it is well to keep in mind that the cult or the problem, whichever way one wants to phrase it, of youth in politics has been very much a product of the 1960s. In 1960 it occurred to practically no one that the Democratic candidate for president, because he was forty-three, was in any sense a candidate or a representative of the young *vs.* the middle-aged. After all, no one had thought in such terms of Mr. Dewey in 1944, then still younger, and running for the office in the middle of a war fought by young men. Nor was the thirty-nine year old vice-presidential candidate of the Republican Party in 1952 selected with the hope that thereby the ticket would appeal to the youth of the nation. Strange as it must sound today, youth, including all our college students, were not, prior to 1960, thought of as a special constituency, a pressure group, a class with its own culture and point of view.

That it should have been so was a natural and logical consequence of democracy. Hence it is not surprising that

Britain and the U.S. had been two societies where there had been no youth problem in the sense in which it has emerged, or, more properly, has been portrayed in recent years. In contrast, the problem of youth in politics has always been a serious one in authoritarian societies and, in a different way, in totalitarian ones. So when people today repeat the famous cliché that student disorders are a world-wide problem, one must add that they have always been so ... except in the United States and Britain, and to a lesser extent in other democratic countries. For indeed how can any democratic theory admit the possibility that a young man, upon reaching the voting age, has any political rights or responsibilities which are different from those of his father?

In a totalitarian state a special cult of youth is, by the same token, very understandable. Once in power or in the process of struggling for it, a totalitarian movement will devote special attention to the young: the middle-aged will grow tired and disillusioned with ideological bathos, weary of constant calls for sacrifice, vigilance, and of irksome regulations; the young, if properly indoctrinated and controlled, will not. Mussolini's Fascism had the "Hymn to Youth" as its official anthem. Who will forget pictures of the *Hitler-jugend* in their Nuremburg encampments, hailing the *Fuehrer* rapturously? Stalin's cruel task of human engineering, the forced collectivization which claimed so many victims, could have been carried through not only because the despot had the police at his disposal, but also because of the undoubted enthusiasm of the Communist youth who took little heed of the human suffering involved in it.*

---

*The classic propaganda tale in Russia in the 1930s was that of a twelve year old peasant boy, Pavlik Morozov, who denounced his parents to the Secret Police for withholding grain from the state. The older Morozovs met the usual fate of the people accused of such a crime, whereas the boy's uncle throttled the little monster. He subsequently was canonized as a Communist hero and martyr, an example to be admired and emulated by all right-thinking Soviet boys and girls.

Attempts to create a youth cult or culture have, of course, not been absent in this society. But until recently they were being observed by Madison Avenue rather than by academicians. Sociologists who write learned disquisitions on rock festivals and their momentous significance scorn the comparison with Frank Sinatra's cult among bobby-soxers of some three decades ago. But why? A look at some movies in the 1950s (*e.g.*, James Dean) will readily demonstrate that Hollywood was trying to sell alienation of the young long before anybody there ever heard of Dr. Herbert Marcuse. Elvis Presley must appear low-brow as against the Beatles, but that is only because he "peaked" at the wrong time when no one thought of linking rock music with the cruelties of post-industrial society and misdeeds of the Establishment. It was about the same time that C. Wright Mills was strenuously expounding the theme which recently has been screaming at us from hundreds of books, articles and television shows: the young and educated have to compensate for their elders' (and the cinema's) disinterest in social change and preoccupation with materialistic values. But who then read C. Wright Mills and, especially, among the young? This remarkable sociologist was to die before his time.

One can go on in this vein, and not only about the U.S. Sartre's tirades about existentialism were, in the late '50s something of a joke among the Paris university youth. Nobody dreamed that he and Simone de Beauvoir would be back in fashion among the ruling deities of the student rebellion of the 1960s. In England one had "angry young men," but the still prevailing censorship and convention prevented too clear an elucidation in the theater or film as to exactly why they were so angry.

It was this past decade which, in today's parlance, put it all together. Until then, efforts to manufacture a youth culture in a democracy suffered from the fact that, unlike in a totalitarian country, you could not coordinate various bodies and agencies of society in one vast propaganda effort. A movie actor or a rock singer might unknowingly serve as a symbol of alienation, but before sociologists would become interested and certify him as such, Hollywood and Madison Avenue would move on to another hero and another theme. Elvis Presley's and C. Wright Mills' constituencies were, as I have said, quite separate. Can one truly say the same about those of Bob Dylan and Herbert Marcuse? Among politicians, no one had thought, in those distant days, of extolling, damning, or imploring the youth, or of cultivating sideburns as a discreet gesture of sympathy with the more moderate of the "now generation." To be sure, one always had those messages to the young about the "challenges" awaiting them, but those were part of the immemorial ritual, like, say, greetings to Americans of Lithuanian extraction on the occasion of the Lithuanian national holiday.

Now, the accent on youth which emanated from the Kennedy administration reflected clearly the academic background of so many of its members as well as the president's own personality. That this emphasis contributed to the youth cult of the 1960s, there is no doubt. It is hardly necessary to add that the president and his advisers can hardly be saddled with the responsibility for the full extent of the cult or some of its lamentable consequences. It took the unhappy turn in the Vietnam War and the generally faltering direction of the nation's affairs after 1963 to produce the deplorable condition of our young, our schools and universities which we have faced. But it is from Washington that there was flashed first the message that the young had "special responsibilities" in politics, that they were the repository of "idealism." The president's celebrated challenge for the citizen to think what he can do for his country rather than what the country can do for him was also addressed primarily to the same group. No one could quarrel with the sentiment or rhetoric. But in the days ahead many would find it difficult just to obey the laws of the land.

There were, however, no somber reflections among the academic community at this highest point of its rise in prestige and influence. If one lived in Cambridge, Massachusetts, one could easily believe that part of its university complex had moved to the shores of the Potomac. The number of those leaving Harvard and M.I.T. for Washington was not overwhelming, and for many of them the change meant simply less frequent commuting between the two cities. But the link between the university and government was now both closer and more explicit. The academic people were now, in many cases, on top as well as on tap. Those who were left behind could share in a feeling of excitement, smile condescendingly at the newspapermen's (as usual) not quite correct stories about the academic background of the new potentates, and keep *au courant* of the social and political news at the highest level not, as hitherto, from the gossip columns but from some of the people *directly* involved. There were, to be sure, those who were envious and resentful, but it took several years before they could give vent to such feelings, when Vietnam had tarnished the laurels of some of the heroes of 1961. At the time, however, one does not recall any voices warning the academicians not to exchange the peace and security of their classrooms and laboratories for the illusion of power and the glitter of Washington cocktail parties. No Cassandras arose conjuring up the picture of the university in strife as a retribution for its presumption. Even in more prosaic terms it would have been reasonable to anticipate some trouble: by acquiring at least the appearance of power the university would inevitably, in the future, become a target of criticism and public hostility. When the Great Depression came, how many were inclined to absolve big business from any share of the responsibility and to claim that the Mellons and the Morgans just happened to be there when things went astray?

The excitement was strongest among the faculty. Insofar as the students were concerned, one does not recall their reactions to the election of 1960 as being markedly different from those in 1956 or 1952. When the president-elect visited Harvard he was received courteously. His urbanity and especially his sense of humor were eventually to secure John F. Kennedy great popularity among the college population; but that there was any special cult of him among the young, or that many of them felt they could, in the language of the late '60s, "relate" to the president, is a subsequent reconstruction verging on a legend. In fact, as one progresses in the decade one feels increasingly the synthetic character of many of the phenomena and characteristics attributed to the young, one learns to suspect statements beginning with "The young are. . . ."

THERE IS NO QUESTION, however, that increasing "governmentalization" of the university, as we might call it, was bound to lead to its politicization. Again, it is no coincidence that Britain and the U.S., the two countries which, until recently, have been most free of chronic, traditional student troubles have also been the ones where higher education has *not* been controlled by the central government, and where the universities, while playing a vast role in public life, did not directly mix in politics. Oxford and Cambridge have for centuries educated Britain's rulers; but the two venerable centers never presumed to rule, in the sense of their faculties assuming a special role vis-à-vis the government. In the United States the enhanced role of the universities—and the fact that some professors have occasionally served as presidential advisers and *confidants (e.g.,* Professor Felix Frankfurter of the Harvard Law School in the 1930s)—never quite thrust a university as a whole in a political role. Suddenly that autumn, in 1961, there was the illusion that Harvard and, in some sense, the university community as a whole, was called upon to share in the government of the United States. An illusion, to be sure, but in the realm of social action and thought, widely held illusions can become as important as facts. Public attention was of necessity riveted on the fact that at least two of the president's special assistants, and three heads of the major diplomatic missions (etc.) had been recruited from the faculty of one university. This was not counting the so-called prominent alumni in the Cabinet and other important positions. The *Harvard Alumni Bulletin* noted coyly under its news of the class of 1940 that John F. Kennedy had moved into the house once inhabited by Franklin D. Roosevelt (class of '04). One grew quite used to phenomena like a Harvard official occupying a rather modest position in its administrative structure being suddenly transferred to a federal post responsible for the disbursement of billions. At the intermediate and lower levels in Washington one had a corresponding influx of bright young men from major university centers.

This migration represented, as yet, only what we called "governmentalization" rather than politicization of the university. Although the character of the new administration was liberal, it was by no means so in any doctrinaire or ritualistic sense of the term. It then seemed to correspond to the mood of many of the politically-minded members of the academic world. Radicalism was then still quite unfashionable. It brought memories of how the fellow travellers had not only been duped, but subsequently made to look ridiculous by the Communists own revelations following Stalin's death. In the domestic sphere, postwar prosperity and what was then considered a serious advance in civil rights acted similarly to undercut the strength of radical phraseology. If radicalism was viewed as old-fashioned, then conservatism never counted many articulate representatives in the academic world any more than in the American intellectual community at large. The new administration thought of itself as "liberal" largely in the sense of being more sympathetic and brainy than Mr. Eisenhower's. Its liberalism did not include that criticism of the U.S. postwar world responsibilities which was to become such an important part of ritualistic liberalism a few years later, nor its equally important ingredient, that masochistic appraisal of the values and reality of what used to be known as the American way of life. Nor did such feelings enjoy, as yet, a wide currency in the academic community. The government and politics oriented segment of it had been involved after all in the sharp internationalist turn of U.S. policies during and after the war, and provided planners and officials for the vast network of aid and international cooperation agencies. That group, while not sharing either J. Edgar Hoover's or John Foster Dulles' view of Communism, still would have found ludicrous any suggestion that the U.S. policies throughout the world could be compared to those of the USSR, or classified in any sense as "imperialist." And since the U.S. role in the world was still thought to be fairly virtuous, there was as yet little incentive to discover grave sins or crimes attributable to American society. After all, before the president-elect announced his other appointments he felt constrained to declare that Messrs. J. Edgar Hoover and Allen Dulles would retain their posts as heads of the F.B.I. and the C.I.A., respectively. There could be little question of all those "professors" turning the ship of state to the left more than would have been the case in any other instance of the Democrats succeeding the Republicans in control of the executive branch. In foreign affairs the new rulers expected to be recognized as "progressive," thereby gaining trust of the Third World; but also (to use that awful journalistic expression) as "tough minded," thus impressing Moscow and other Communist powers with America's stern resolve.

ENOUGH HAS BEEN SAID, then, to dispel any suggestion that the great professorial migration to Washington meant in any sense an influx of "subversive" ideas, that the newcomers were "soft on Communism." There could be no justification for any of those formulas which are used by the right-wing to bewail the influence of the academic, or the intellectual, world in general on politics. The danger and the eventual harm in the government getting too mixed up with the university lay elsewhere. Precisely because the university had attained such great importance in and for society, one should have been careful to keep it at an arm's length from politics. The fact that they got too much mixed up with each other was to be good for neither.

The dangers inherent in this tie-up were to become apparent already in the backwash of the Bay of Pigs fiasco of the spring of 1961. The Cuban enterprise could have been reasonably criticized on two grounds: that it should never have been attempted in the first place; or that, if attempted, it should not have been planned and executed so ineptly. But the reaction in many university and intellectual circles was of a different kind: How could *this* government have attempted such a thing! Some in those categories professed to find it inconceivable that an administration which contained so many liberal professors should have tried such a sneaky kind of affair. Weren't those representatives of the world of the mind guarantees that this government, unlike those of Messrs. Truman and Eisenhower, would act only out of the purest liberal motives? Others have found in the whole affair a not too displeasing confirmation of their worst fears: hardly three months have passed since the Inauguration and their colleagues had already been hopelessly corrupted by power. The rebuttal by some of those assailed was also instructive. The failure and/or the whole idea of invading Cuba was blamed on "them": the Chiefs of Staff, the C.I.A., the former administration. The president, to his great credit, would brook no such excuses and manfully accepted the ultimate responsibility; but mutual recriminations and accusations went on, and they, even more than the failure of the enterprise itself, were to have a baneful effect on the future course of American foreign policy.

The aftermath of the Bay of Pigs thus demonstrated already one of the basic dilemmas of the government-university tie-up. In theory it should have benefited both sides as well as the public at large. The government benefits through having a large number of experts executing as well as advising on policies; the academic world gets a better grasp of the realities of power, and the country profits if public issues are discussed and explained by people skilled in argument for their profession in education. The aftermath of the first Cuban crisis showed that, unfairly but perhaps not unpredictably, things in the real world don't always work that way. The United States Government made a mistake which governments and individuals are bound to make at times. But this mistake was both magnified and its consequences made more serious by the attempts to rationalize it by implying that the U.S. Government was composed, so to speak, of two parts—the nimble and virtuous part, *i.e.*, the president and most of his political advisers, and the rather stupid and sinister one, *i.e.*, the military, the C.I.A., etc. The academic critic of politics, for his part, became much more critical because this to him was not simply a case of the U.S. Government committing an error or being immoral, but one of betrayal. As to the lessons and consequences flowing out of the failure, the public instead of being enlightened became only confused because of the character of the debate. One could see in the whole affair some of those elements which were to contribute to the unhappy decisions on Vietnam and to weigh even more heavily on the unfortunate reactions to those decisions. In their interaction the academic person and the politician appear at times to exchange their traditional roles, the former becoming ambitious to demonstrate how tough and free from ideological scruples he is, the other tending to become doctrinaire as if bent upon showing his academic colleague that he too understood and cared about the world of ideas. Is there some mysterious law ordaining that a too close association between the government and the university is bound to reveal the weakest sides of each?

In retrospect, in the early 1960s the American university looms like an impregnable fortress dominating not only the cultural but the social landscape of America. The successive waves of invaders, right-wing obscurantists, left-wing zealots, McCarthyites, Birchers, *et al.*, had beaten at its gates but had been repulsed. Now they had been reduced to small ineffectual groups skirmishing in the neighborhood and utterly incapable of a frontal assault. But precisely at this point, several columns were approaching from separate directions which, in an assault in the mid-60s, would join and then, with amazing ease, breach the walls.

One such force was the youth cult. In a way it was always present on the American scene, based on those incontrovertible and eternal truths that the young, as a rule, are more attractive, impetuous, and deserving of attention and understanding than their elders. But it never had political implications. Now it was to be stimulated in that direction by politicians looking for novel slogans. The theme was to be picked up by mass media, Madison Avenue and then, somewhat belatedly, discovered by radicals. But it was to take a foolishly conceived and even more foolishly conducted war for the young themselves to become imbued with the cult and for a sizeable proportion of college students to let themselves be persuaded by sociologists, preachers, and advertisers that they were virtually a new biological species, the first generation endowed with complete selflessness and idealism. Once this belief attained the proportions of a national cult, the university administrators and faculties would find themselves in a virtually impossible situation. They were, by their own admission, sinful and old or middle-aged and yet claiming to exercise authority over the virtuous youth. Where, then, was the whole rationale of rules, examinations and, more fundamentally, of the principle that the young have to learn from them rather than vice versa? This was to become known as the problem of "legitimacy."

"Relevance" was to be the device of yet another group of assailants. Here we have a clear causal relationship between the prosperity and prestige of the early 1960s and the troubles of the late years of the decade. The university was revealed (well, *some* universities anyway) as a desirable even glamorous place to be. It was then palpably unfair and undemocratic that it should be monopolized just by scholars and teachers. It was as if it suddenly became known that in an abandoned territory, fit perhaps for an Indian reservation, there were precious mineral deposits. The influx of people without the traditional credentials and interests could be rationalized mainly on the ground that the university's function was much broader than just expanding and passing on knowledge.

The American university, unlike its European or British counterpart, could never be accused of scorning the practical. But for all the schools of agriculture, business, and home economics, it was always recognized that the core of instruction and interest in any university worthy of its name had to be academic in the proper sense of the word. But now, the pressures of the university to do something other than what its purpose implies, and what are the only things it can do well, were bound to be multiplied manifold. A man, by profession or temperament, a bureaucrat, politician, or social reformer, who found himself on the faculty, was bound to feel (often with the best motivation possible) that the traditional academic attitudes and concerns were old-fashioned if not outright anti-democratic. Wasn't it narrow pedantry and intellectual snobbery which ruled when it came to most faculty appointments, the student's curriculum, and so on? The university cared but little for the pressing problems of the community in which it was situated. It took but "academic" interest in the social and ethical issues confronting society at large. If he felt less qualified intellectually than the traditional scholar, then the new type of faculty member felt more useful or, as in a few years he would say, more relevant. To the already sizeable and growing cadre of people with mainly administrative interests and duties was now being added a not inconsiderable number of people whose ambitions ran toward politics or social engineering, and who a few years before would have, in some cases, found themselves in politics or a bureaucracy of one sort or another. But now, since the university was so much in the public eye, one could be in politics while attached to a school, or one could expound one's pet theories conscious that they would cause reverberations in Washington or at the local level. In brief, one did not have to abandon the exciting world of affairs and withdraw from public attention by taking a job in Cambridge, Massachusetts, New Haven, or Berkeley, often quite the contrary.

A sprinkling of such operators (as the new breed became known) could be useful and enlivening. But once a critical mean was reached, the university, especially in its social science branches, would run the danger of being deflected from its proper course. That very desirable parochialism which characterized the atmosphere of the university was already shaken by the example of those who had gone to Washington; and it was further undermined by Washington and the outside world, so to speak, coming to the university to display their allurements. Serving the public interest, *i.e.,* being relevant, was *then* almost synonymous with serving or advising (whether asked or unasked) the government and the powers that be. But the operator was to show himself a hardy and adaptable breed. Came the time when dissent became fashionable and many an operator turned into an agitator! Trips to Washington were replaced by appearances at "teach-ins" and protest rallies. Those memoranda to the high and mighty gave way to paperbacks and articles expounding innovative ideas and the new imperatives of a coming revolution. A few even managed to do both. . . . Relevance, then, was the further stage and outgrowth of this expansion of policy studies of which I spoke before. To be sure, as we shall see later on, the movement was to grow more tumultuous and wide. And, as we shall also see, the whole pressure to make academic studies "relevant" was not only to deal a blow to the university, but to have results contrary to its professed aim. Just as by emphasizing applied science at the expense of pure research, so by attempting to make the university *directly* useful to the problem of society, we can only damage and curtail that vast beneficent but indirect usefulness which it has if it keeps to its proper job.

TODAY THE APOSTLES of relevance and of the youth cult are virtually indistinguishable from each other. And they have been joined by a previously separate detachment of analysts and sociologists. It is not unusual to find today in one and the same book or article a ringing denunciation of our society for its encouragement of the competitive mania, praise for the youth for its virtuous indignation and rejection of false idols, criticism of education as based on outworn concepts, and the assertion that these insights are not mere opinions but fruits of dispassionate scientific study. But in the early years of the decade, it was still somewhat unusual for an analyst or sociologist to assume and proclaim that his professional expertise entitled him to scientific verdicts on Vietnam, the ABM, or the Middle East crisis. Since the disciples of Freud already manned so many commanding heights in the university and the American intellectual establishment, their accession to the forces of dissent and relevance was to be perhaps decisive in the success those forces were to achieve.

No question, then, that the excessive profusion of courses on motivation, group dynamics, and personality was to contribute to the future crisis. One does not wish to follow the anti-Freudian zealot who would ban teachings of the Viennese master and their offshoots on grounds that just as Indians to alcohol, so the Americans are unduly susceptible to gloomy introspection (witness Puritanism) and should not be allowed additional stimuli.* But one may plead for balance and a sense of proportion. The profusion of those courses led many, especially the college student, to devote the bulk of his time not to the study of English literature or mathematics, but to the study of himself as seen by some luminaries of the Freudian establishment. That, one submits, was not what Socrates meant by his famous injunction—that the Athenian youth should lay aside their learning and games to spend time brooding over their assorted hang-ups. From this situation there was but one step to the unspoken premise of so many today that all of education should be, in fact, a form of group therapy. But why blame the young? Our whole society seems to have taken to the couch trying to recall the reason for its trauma. What was it—was it the way it treated the Indian, or the mad pursuit of material goals, or perhaps the automobile? Alienation and the identity crisis

---

*Such has been the fate of psychoanalysis in the Soviet Union where its prohibition is justified because of its alleged conflict with Marxism, its alleged aim to persuade the individual to find reasons for his unhappiness within himself rather than in his capitalist environment. Why, might one ask then, are the blessings of psychoanalysis denied to inhabitants of a *Communist* country in which the individual is instructed precisely that if he is unhappy it cannot be on account of the system under which he lives? Here one can only speculate that the Soviets must feel that the needs of the citizens of the U.S.S.R. to confess and inform are amply provided for by an agency of the state.

ride grimly through most of contemporary culture, through literature, theater, and cinema, claiming victims among those who refuse to seek salvation in relevance and commitment. Few dare to question premises of the cult. To do so is, of course, only to betray hostility and secret fear which show how badly one needs its ministrations.

SUCH WERE, THEN, the enemy forces approaching the seemingly impregnable, proud, and prosperous American university. At first they could hardly be identified as such. Relevance was not yet fully discovered: its primitive forms, speaking in quasi-biological terms, could be found in such phenomena as I noted before, *e.g.*, complaints that "research" was being overemphasized at the expense of "teaching." Here and there an assistant professor who was not promoted to a permanent faculty rank would complain that he was being penalized for his concern for the students which made him eschew those pedantic pursuits that go under the name of research in favor of teaching (and what is currently known as "interaction"). Sometimes their protests were endorsed by students, and sometimes they were even justified.

Another straw in the wind was the obvious and growing restlessness of young men and women who attended colleges under the rules and regulations designed to govern their conduct as imposed and administered by the colleges. This restlessness is traditional and immemorial, but the reasons for it were novel. Traditionally, college students have felt oppressed by such rules, whether those stipulating certain dress codes or (and especially) ordaining hours and conditions and manner under which students may entertain those of a different sex. But this grievance was usually felt on personal rather than ideological grounds. Let us note one side-effect of the (strict) parietal rules which a psychologist may deem beneficial rather than otherwise: the students were encouraged to believe that their social and/or sexual failures could be blamed on the college rather than on themselves or their parents. In any case in most schools, certainly at Harvard, the formerly idiotically strict parietal rules had been eroded by the sixties to sensibly hypocritical proportions.

But here was the rub; the new protest gathering force was, at least we were being so advised by middle-aged exponents of the cause of youth, ideological rather than personal in character. It was not discomfort but the derogation of their dignity that the young resented: those humiliating rules on dress, deportment, intra-sex entertainment. Confronted with this swelling protest movement, college administrations (as they usually do) gave ground. But the way this capitulation was taking place bespoke the future trouble. It was perfectly understandable why some, or most, students should wish to live without any irksome regulations, college officials and proctors, to check on them. But in that case, those desirous of such freedom should have assumed commensurate responsibilities, *i.e.*, finding their own quarters and designing their own amusements. Or, if the investment in college dormitories had been too high for such a step, those dormitories ought to have been turned completely over to the students to be run and managed as cooperatives or what-have-you. In other words, a young person can be treated as an adult or as not quite an adult. But in their desire to please, and to appease, the college administrators were evolving a third category. Insofar as his demeanor, obligations and account of residence, and the like, were concerned, the college student began to claim and obtain rights and indulgences not possessed by the adult unconnected with the university, and without much of the latter's obligations both before the law and when it comes to sheer management of one's own affairs. A peculiar form of paternalism was, then evolving in many of the colleges: a growing army of officials to administer a constantly diminishing body of rules. One could often admire their solicitude for the young, sympathize with their desire to be popular with the latter, but all along one suspected that the whole approach was unsound, at once permissive and patronizing. And such an approach could inspire neither trust nor respect.

POLITICAL RADICALISM was an infrequent visitor on the university scene until the middle 1960s. Activism on behalf of civil rights, prominent among students at the time, certainly could not be identified with any specific ideological affiliation. It attracted adherents, as it should have, among all shades of political opinion excepting the extreme reactionaries. Neither of the two Cuban crises of 1961 and 1962 created any specific campus or university community reactions markedly different from those felt in the country at large. There was a subtle transition in the attitude toward Fidel Castro. At first, the highbrow view of him was one of condescending humor: radicalism when accompanied by a beard and endless oratory could not be treated too seriously especially coming from a man who himself confessed that he never got beyond page 300 of Vol. I of *Capital*. But the discomfiture he was causing the United States and his certification as a genuine revolutionary by Sartre and C. Wright Mills had, by 1962, earned him a small coterie of academic followers. Yet when, in 1962, a very personable and popular Harvard professor ran for the Senate as a third party candidate and on a platform strongly critical of U.S. foreign policy, he failed to draw any special youth or academic support.

Political radicalism, in brief, was to be a product of the forces which we described above, plus Vietnam, rather than a spontaneous outburst of political idealism as it has frequently been described. And we may hazard a conjecture that even without Vietnam—or to be more precise, even without the unwisely conceived and foolishly managed American overcommitment in Southeast Asia—those forces damaging to the true interests of the American university would have still grown in strength and wreaked havoc.

The first stage of the troubles in the university might be dubbed the Berkeley phase. This branch of the University of California had been known to have troubles for a long time. Periodically, the administration would run into trouble with the faculty or the regents appointed by the state legislature would have difficulties with the administration *and* faculty. Finally, greater than usual dissension seemed to prevail in many of Berkeley's departments. In a way this seemed nature's way to preserve a balance: without those "troubles" it was difficult to see how the University of California could have failed to become the country's and the world's incomparably best university. Certainly it had all the conceivable and even some inconceivable advantages over its rival institutions. The legislature of what was becoming the biggest and richest state in the union was willing to pour vast sums of money into its leading school. The older and traditionally more prestigious institutions were either in the barren north with frigid winters and unbearably hot summers or in the midst of rapidly deteriorating metropolitan complexes. Berkeley has a magnificent climate and most charming location. The university managed even before the state's great growth to establish an enviable reputation and to assemble a distinguished faculty. In brief, it seemed the envy of gods which ordained that an institution with so many natural advantages should experience so many difficulties so that it remained *one* of the best rather than *the* best university in the country.

Here, in 1964, occurred the first major explosion on the university campus of America. The crisis was on. Television crews and newspapermen rushed to the scene, sociologists to their cubicles to produce learned analyses. The president of the whole network of institutions which was the University of California and of which Berkeley was just one (though the most distinguished) component was at the time one of the leading educational statesmen in the country. Educational statesmen before 1965 were what educational reformers or educators are now: people expected to deliver speeches and addresses assessing the past, appraising the present, welcoming the various challenges of the future. The gentleman in question had just delivered such a series of lectures at Harvard, where he coined a new term for the university in the brave new world taking shape: "Multiversity." The times seemed to be propitious for such neologisms and new concepts: witness the laurels worn by the discoverers of the "identity crisis," of "inner motivation," etc. But alas! *multiversity* was coined at one of those turning points in history, when something that was safe and even laudable before, suddenly and inexplicably becomes dangerous and scandalous. The rebelling students and the discontented faculty members could not at first find a simple formula and target for their wrath, but then somebody remembered *multiversity* so incautiously presented to them by their own president. The word, from describing the magnificent vista of the future, of the university extending its tentacles in every direction and, nourished by federal funds, growing ever bigger, came to be associated with an inhuman monster swallowing lively (and so full of promise and creativity) young men and women and attempting to turn them into puppet-like servants of the military-industrial establishment. This was before Vietnam took on major proportions. (President Johnson, then in the middle of his campaign and obviously destined to be triumphantly successful, kept assuring that he had no intention of sending "American boys" to do the job which was up to the "Asian boys," as he rather quaintly put it.) Relevance was still to raise its head. Hence it was Multiversity which had to serve as the most convenient target for the pent-up fury of the young, and for that not inconsiderable discontent and frustration which their elders had accumulated.

The events at Berkeley were to provide much of the scenario for future troubles at other universities. Agitated discussion among the faculty, with those strange flashes of bitterness of feeling and rage on the part of people one always assumed had been engrossed in their own work and hardly aware of the world outside their study and classroom; the strange proneness of so many people, professors and students alike, to see in the administrators of the university, for the most part men of good will and no more bumbling or pompous than any other bureaucrats, embodiments of hateful and repressive authority; and, finally, the readiness and the delusion of the belief that peace could be purchased by "restructuring," through new committees, through a "dialogue" with those who were rebelling and as yet did not quite know why.

One incident deserves to be recalled, for the future historian may mark it as one of those moments in history when the old world gives way to the new, when the American university of rules and authority breathed its last days. A debate was held before a large audience to discuss youth's discontent and its remedies. At one point one of the most eminent leaders of the student rebellion interrupted the proceedings and started shouting. Thereupon policemen emerged from the wings of the stage where they had hidden and dragged off the protester. The chairman of the meeting (an eminent political scientist rumored *before* the incident as being considered for one of the high administrative positions which lately had become vacant) was subsequently questioned as to why he allowed this brute display of force, rather than, as was to become the cunning administrative practice on such occasions, "playing it cool" and allowing the man to discredit himself. He answered in words which posterity may compare in significance and insensitivity with

Marie Antoinette's "let-them-eat-cake." He said, "This was to be a structured meeting." So many things in American university life were soon to become utterly unstructured.

Bertolt Brecht, the famous Communist poet, when pressured about Stalin's purges, is reputed to have delivered himself of the aphorism: "The victim is always guilty." This sentiment marked much of the reaction to the events at Berkeley. Since the issue (a fateful word soon to resound incessantly on every campus) was, along with the "multiversity," the freedom of speech and political propaganda, the university senate authorized the fullest student freedom in that respect. Pressured by the faculty's as well as students' wrath, the old insensitive university officials were replaced by new, responsive ones. Yet the Berkeley troubles continued.

The news media, at first, treated the Berkeley events with certain avuncular condescension. This was but a longer than usual student caper vaguely analogous to those yearly and boisterous student descents on Fort Lauderdale, or those wild debutante parties of recent memories where the young guests ended up by wrecking their hosts' homes. Then, there was always something new and mad coming out of California. But soon came the realization that this could be not a caper but the beginning of a trend, not a mere outburst of youthful frivolity or impetuosity but evidence of deep social malaise. Some years later when Harvard, in turn, was under siege, I happened to walk in front of the building where the faculty was holding an emergency meeting which, it had been rumored, was going to be invaded by student radicals. Several television trucks were parked in front of the building, their crews watching with disgust the empty square: the radicals did not come. . . .

Similarly at other universities, the Berkeley drama was treated at one time as yet another of those visitations which that institution had to endure for its unfair advantages. An undergraduate acquaintance of mine asked a question which revealed a Machiavellian turn of mind worthy of a member of the Soviet secret police: Was it true that at the first inkling of troubles in California, Harvard had dispatched emissaries to tempt some of the most prominent professorial luminaries to forsake sunny but disturbed California for less sunny but serene Cambridge, Massachusetts? That such ridiculously sinister rumors could be believed by intelligent young men was a manifestation of that deep suspiciousness which characterizes the mind of the young, and evidence of what strange notions prevailed among them concerning academic customs and procedures.

Some faculty members were, however, by 1965 beginning to leave the embattled university. It was not as yet realized that a motto for American higher education in the next five years could be borrowed from the title of a book on the dangers of nuclear war: no place to hide. The escapees were bringing with them tales of a considerable political strife which had engulfed the faculty in the West Coast university and of bizarre goings on within the student body.

Here a digression is necessary. University politics prior to the above and lamentable developments had seldom been political in the real sense of the word with the Left and the Right, liberal and conservative factions confronting each other. No, it usually turned on disagreement and generally harmless intrigues concerning purely academic developments, appointments, and the like, where disputes and hostility reached across political lives. Similarly with the students, if they thought of college regulations, courses, and similar aspects of their university existence, it was again in non-political terms and a Communist student might find himself allied to a conservative one in trying to change or repeal certain regulations. There had been, then, a common-sense recognition that differences of views on most problems concerning the university had little to do with political distinctions, that whether one was radical, liberal, or conservative had but little to do with one's notions of the university, the way it should operate, the students' rights and privileges. With California things began to change.

WHAT WAS TO HAPPEN during the next five years was to be best explained in a brilliant, if unconscious, insight revealed by a student at the commencement exercises at Radcliffe in 1969. The young lady tried to explain the apparent paradox of students like herself, greatly fond of their institution and yet at the same time constrained, as happened just before at Harvard-Radcliffe, to wreak havoc. The reason was simple: the university was the only institution which was responsive to the anguish and violence of sensitive young women and men. Other institutions failed to respond to or even notice protest and dissent. The university was almost always more obliging. So what else could they do but strike against it? Most people spend most of their lives, observed another American philosopher some time ago, in quiet desperation. It remains quiet, we might add, because those people realize that if they gave vent to their exasperation it would be, in today's phrase, counter-productive. But in the mid-60s it was suddenly discovered that there was one place which miraculously fitted the requisite of every man's ill humor. The university was elitist; it debased learning by letting in utterly unqualified people. It permitted, nay encouraged, promiscuity and the use of drugs; it repressed the young. It advised the Pentagon and big business how to meddle in the affairs of other nations; it bred anti-patriotic feelings and anarchism. It epitomized white supremacy; it stimulated black radicalism and separatism. It was a repository of useless pedantry; it was full of busybodies who, under the pretense of objective study of society, sought power and were eager to submit their fellow citizens to some half-baked schemes of their fabrication. And by 1969 one had to admit that there was an element of truth in *all* those charges!

The repercussions of Vietnam were to weigh heavily on the college scheme but it would not be correct to blame them for the developments just mentioned. Rather, the war illuminated the weaknesses of the American university, and hastened but did not originate the intense phase of its crisis.

The idiocy of the draft law which exempted university students while at the same time something like half-a-million of their contemporaries found themselves in a war zone has been sufficiently commented on. It would also be superfluous to expound on the psychological effects of so many young people being torn between feelings of guilt and fear. The university became a safe but somewhat shameful haven, and it is not surprising, quite apart from any other plausible causes, why many university students tried to resolve their inner conflict through strong feelings of indignation about the war. But why should that feeling have manifested itself in, through, and against the university? Here, if the answer is to be given not in terms of rhetoric and clichés (the university's complicity, the polarization of academic life, the students' idealism) but of actual causes, one must try to reconstruct the sequence of events.

The bombings of North Vietnam in February 1965 may not have scared the North Vietnamese; but, to paraphrase the Duke of Wellington's saying about his troops, they certainly scared us. From Mr. Walter Lippmann to, it seems safe to say, circles within the administration, everyone pondered what "they" (*i.e.,* the Russians and/or the Chinese) would do. This speculation was enhanced by the Soviets' ominous if vague hints (usual in such cases) of horrendous things to come if the Americans would not stop unprecedented (and it was that) interference with and reaction to Communist infiltration and subversion. The bombings then, it is important to realize, produced a severe shock which has not worn off entirely even now. Without them, it is fair to say, the Americans' presence in Vietnam, say on the order of 100,000 troops, would not have produced one tenth of the kind of reaction our actual involvement has led to at home and abroad.

First, then, came fear, and not a moralistic critique of America's policies. And in the era of the ICBM and the hydrogen bomb who can blame the people for being fearful? Then came a rapid increase in the numbers of Americans fighting, or at least garrisoned, in South Vietnam.

We cannot be concerned here with the details of the debate on Vietnam nor with the administration's less than frank, perhaps not quite clear and comprehensible, exposition of the reason why we were so much involved there. Let me note at once that the very beginning of the debate on Vietnam showed the damage inflicted by that too close involvement of the American university with the federal government which we have called governmentalization. Where could we get an objective assessment of America's posture in Vietnam, its advantages and risks, the soundness or error of the premises on which that policy was based, of the means employed? The proverbial well-informed layman could not begin to appreciate the complexities of the issue, could not decide whether he was to follow Mr. Walter Lippmann's gloomy apprehensions or to trust Mr. Joseph Alsop's euphoric approval. Theoretically a reasoned analysis could come only from the university. But from the beginning it was very clear that there were few scholars who were not *"engagé,"* whether professionally or emotionally or both, on the issue of U.S. foreign policy and especially in Southeast Asia. Without ascribing any ignoble motivations to those concerned, it was only human that the people involved in our policy-making, either officials or advisers, were hardly capable of an objective appraisal and neither were those who felt rancor, legitimate or otherwise, at *not* being officials or advisers. The initial phase of Vietnam was already a vivid demonstration of how seriously diminished was the practical use of the university, precisely because it was *not* more detached from policy-making, because it was not more of an "ivory tower."

On Vietnam, as on many issues of vast national importance, the university failed to be a lobby for reason. Arguments advanced by scholars, whether *pro* or *con*, became more rather than less tinged with emotionalism than those employed by politicians. Fairly early in the debate Mr. Arthur Schlesinger, Jr. wrote wisely, "It is not only idle but unfair to seek out guilty men" (*i.e.,* for our overcommitment) and "let us never forget that complicated problems can be resolved only by reasoned analysis."* In fact, from the beginning the debate centered around the question "who is guilty" rather than on what were the facts.

The very format of the debate promised from the beginning to contribute more to passion than to understanding. Intellectual debate cannot thrive in an atmosphere of a trial, or that of a televised entertainment. One of the earlier encounters matched the then special assistant on security affairs to President Johnson, McGeorge Bundy, versus a renowned student of American foreign policy, Professor Hans Morgenthau. Each of the contestants was assisted by two academic aides. The debate did not lack elements of personal acrimony. Listeners could presumably form their own conclusions as to who was a more skillful debater. But there was something basically wrong in the whole juxtaposition: Mr. Bundy's role was that of an adviser on and executor of policies, Professor Morgenthau's was that of an analyst and critic. The university was supposed to be

---

*Arthur Schlesinger, Jr., *The Bitter Heritage: Vietnam and American Democracy 1941-1966* (Boston: Houghton Mifflin, 1967), pp. 31, 126.

the place where policies were analysed, the government where they were made. Here the university community was already being put in an adversary position *vis-à-vis* the government, a relationship as unhealthy as collusion between the two. Or, to be more precise, part of the university community was placed in the position of a servant and another of an enemy of the administration, not on account of their respective political views which, of course, would be proper, but because of their alleged professorial expertise. The day was not far away when two equally eminent physicists would take diametrically opposed stands on whether the U.S. should deploy the ABM and whether it was of any use. But what could be the conclusion of a layman, especially if he realized that one eminent scientist was in the employ of the government while the other was an adviser of an opposition senator? On almost every issue engaging public attention and national concern, whether on drugs or on the most efficacious ways of ending discrimination in education, one has been treated to a similar spectacle. We live in the day of the expert. The average citizen has been bullied to the point where he dare not have his own opinion on matters which not so long ago were thought susceptible to common sense judgment. To do so—to be confident of one's own opinion on children's upbringing, violence, drugs—is to be anti-intellectual and indeed to incur the suspicion of being a secret follower of Vice-President Agnew! Yet experts themselves disagree, and they are supposed to do so according to the ideology or rather ideological fashions they follow. Witness the universal surprise and the shock to the forces of dissent when a man with credentials as progressive as Dr. Spock adjudged pot and pornography to be *harmful*!

The very beginning of the Vietnam debate, thus, illuminated dramatically how "engaged" much of our scholarship, so many of our scholars have already become. It was inevitable, though unfair, that the university as well as the government would become a victim of the celebrated credibility gap. But the voice of scholarship was to grow not only increasingly partisan but also strident, if not hysterical. Then, soon, began teach-ins, combinations of debate and endurance-contests reminiscent of the celebrated dance marathons of the 1930s. The fashion swept the campuses of the nation. It was unclear, perhaps even to their sponsors, what exactly was the rationale behind those weird and unendurably lengthy exercises. Was it supposed to be a form of intellectual self-flagellation in expiation of the sins being committed by the United States in Southeast Asia? Were people at the end of ten or twelve hours of listening and talking to be stricken with some sudden illumination, or was it to jar young people from their already considerable state of uncertainty and anxiety into outright hysteria? If it was the last, then it had the desired effect.

That important political issues of the day should be discussed on the campus is both proper and desirable. But it is a different (and in a democracy) most undesirable situation when the university campus becomes the *center* of such a political debate. That it should have become so in regard to Vietnam was in no sense the result of a spontaneous student reaction, nor was it, as is also alleged, the work of the "campus radicals." Like most youth movements, this one was instigated and guided, in its first stages at least, by middle-aged men. Agitation among the faculty communicated itself to the students and resulted in what was to be described as "activism." In an amazingly short time it was assumed by almost everybody to be perfectly natural for the college campus to reverberate to every development and turn on the national political scene. So much so that those interludes when a presidential speech, or a new twist in the tragedy of Vietnam, failed to bring about some violent student demonstration or worse were ascribed (by some regretfully, by others with relief) to the return of "student apathy!" Or, as a colleague confided to me, *his* students must be "apathetic" for they attended all his classes, scrupulously read all the books he assigned.

The reason that the university should have become the focus first of agitation over, then of opposition to Vietnam policies of Mr. Johnson's administration is fairly obvious. Many within the academic community have come to regard the government of the United States as in a peculiar sense "their" government, obligated to adhere to their criteria, meet their expectations, and to weigh their opinions, individually and collectively, over and above those of people in other walks of life. This, for the most part, unconscious elitism was responsible for the fact that many a disgruntled professor chose to express his disagreement with national policies not politically but academically, not by supporting those politicians who opposed our escalation of the war at that point and in his capacity as a *mere* citizen, but by loosing thunderbolts of his *expert* wrath from a university platform. Some simply sought an audience to communicate their anguish and disillusionment and found it most easily in their students. Others craved attention which could not be secured by a letter to the local newspaper or even the *New York Times* but in their early phase could be procured by a dramatic stance at a teach-in. But, whatever the reason, a considerable number of people sought to express their political unhappiness within the precincts of the university rather than in a city auditorium, appealing to the students rather than the electorate. And many of those who indulged in such activities were to be horrified when confronted with the students' demonstrations, seizures, and demands. They had meant to stir up the students against certain policies but not against the government of the United States, and certainly not against their university.

The charge that the university or academicians were in any special sense "responsible for Vietnam" was raised a bit later

and, of course, was extremely silly. How can whole
professions any more than whole nations be held responsible
for errors or sins of a few? But if there was no real justice
then there was an element of what is known as poetic justice
in the charge. As our academic heroes set forth for
Washington in the early 1960s, they were accompanied by
admiration, or what is another term for it, secret envy of
many of their colleagues, with the exception of those
hopelessly misanthropic or completely lost in their work. The
profession as a whole felt raised in prestige and national
significance. Now, as the academicians began to return in the
mid-60s (some quietly, others with loud protestations as to
how their brilliant ideas became distorted by politicians and
bureaucrats), there was bound to be a corresponding and
equally irrational feeling that somehow the university
community as a whole was responsible for getting us into the
whole mess. A Shakespeare scholar from Wabash who had
basked in the reflected glory of a nuclear specialist from
Berkeley would now be viewed by his students as being
somehow responsible for the likelihood of their being
dispatched to Vietnam after their graduation. This, in turn,
tended to make him even more vociferous in his opposition
to U.S. policies, but with the predictable result that without
improving his image in the eyes of the now burgeoning New
Left he was confirming the traditional one in the eyes of the
Old Right. The increasing eagerness of some faculty members
to escape the charges of (the word was just coming into
fashion) *complicity* was to have some tragi-comic effects.
Even in the face of the rising tide of academic criticism, there
was still a fair number of people on the campus rendering aid
and comfort to the government of the United States. More
than that, the great majority of courses taught in economics,
political science and sociology, etc. still carried a tacit or
spoken assumption that there was some reality to American
democracy, that Western civilization favored freedom, that a

two or three party system was desirable and the like. By 1966, it is fair to say, many a sagacious college administrator, many a faculty member, worried about his rapport with his students, was reaching the same conclusion: the university was excessively, in any case imprudently, involved with the government, and committed to the social status quo. But wasn't there a prudent and cunning way of anticipating and forestalling trouble on that account? Activities of the U.S. government were wicked, or undesirable, insofar as they bore on defense and foreign policy. Hence the university would be well advised to curtail and eventually eliminate any research or teaching having to do with that bad part of the federal government. Fortunately this would not mean forswearing federal funds for there was a virtuous side to the U.S. government, one which dispensed monies or scholarships for non-military, non-foreign policy research in social sciences, public health, medicine, etc. For those purposes one could take money even from Washington without compromising the integrity and impartiality of the university. A different stratagem could be employed in connection with the curriculum, slanted as it was being sadly discovered now, too much in the direction of positive evaluation of American institutions and those of Western civilization in general. One could license, perhaps discreetly encourage, courses showing, well, the other side of the coin. An alert college administrator soon had an occasion to congratulate himself if his institution contained a quota of the *right kind* of vociferous radical. The right kind was, of course, one who blamed various social and international ills on the distant powers that be rather than on the university itself. The alumni might sulk at first but the students, ran the secret hope, could not fail to be impressed by such proofs of impartiality and even "commitment" on the part of their Alma Mater. Their rising wrath would be deflected against the Pentagon, against their parents, and spare deans and professors.

Let me hasten to add that this shift and this subtle new policy on the part of so many university officials may have begun as a result of cold calculation, but it soon took the form of conversion. Many in the university community were to feel that they had pursued false gods, whether those of power and influence or of research and publication, and had forgotten the student. Suddenly, *c.* 1966-1967 *students,* disappeared as it were, as a collection of vast numbers of people defying any denominator except of age and their temporary status. Before many an administrator and professor now stood the student, stern and unsmiling, demanding an accounting of what *he* has done with this country, with its foreign policy, soon with the environment, how he has been spending his time and what he proposes to do to expiate his sins. But there was, hopefully, a companion image, that of the *kids,* a generation uniquely unspoiled, devoid of the materialist and competitive passion which has blighted American society; and, instead, devoted to innocent merriment and the ideal of brotherhood. With the kids one could have a dialogue, that is if one discarded sinful attributes of authority, experience, and the like.

Here, then, were the images which found their way to the newspapers, films, literature, and eventually impressed quite a number of young men themselves.

4

The Fall

THE NEW YOUTH CULTURE has been the product of an intensive promotion campaign. For example, its cornerstone, we are told, is the famous sexual revolution. But when did it start? Here the future historian may well be able to fix the date with some precision. In 1966 a national magazine with a faltering circulation ran a feature article on young college couples living together without the benefit, as it is usually described, of a marriage license. Hardly a startling novelty, some might have pointed out. But what *was* relatively new were the names and the rather awkwardly posed pictures of those admitting their illicit bliss and informing, accordingly, the millions of subscribers and casual readers of the magazine in question. Not many years had passed since a president of Vassar had delivered an impassioned defense of virginity as a state entirely appropriate and practicable for young ladies in college. Here now were students challenging not only the obsolete moral code but those hypocritical college administrators who winked at or, with leering condescension, tolerated immorality as long as it did not involve cohabitation. One already had here this rather incongruous mixture of the craving for comfort with the need for a heroic defiance—it was to mark so much of the alleged youth revolt. Furtive, or even not so furtive, lovers' meetings were not enough; what was sought even more than sex was domesticity. The heroic defiance consisted not only in scorning what used to be known as convention, but letting the fact be known to the whole world including parents, deans, and what probably entailed the most risk, prospective new boy and girl friends.

The judicious college officials in whose province it lay to deal with that kind of behavior concluded, undoubtedly, that this was but the latest in youth's never-ending struggle to be noticed and to infuriate their elders. But a year or so later *Life* itself took on the theme of unwedded bliss among students in some of our leading institutions. It did so in a manner so typically its own: this was not sensationalism, trading on sex, or anything of the sort. No, this was a discovery of a previously unnoticed *growing trend* among America's young. One did not have to approve or to castigate this custom, but one *had* to face it, talk about it, discuss possible consequences, ramifications and so on. Names and pictures were again produced, but this time photographs were much better, their subjects blending into the domestic surroundings without that stiffness and posed effect which characterized the pioneering venture. Thus "the honest look at sex in college" had come of age. It coincided with what might be called "we-must-not-sweep-it-under-the-rug" passion which has seized the magazines along with other media and led them to advance boldly into fields previously judged inappropriate for wide public discussion. Nobody could accuse serious media of neglecting to instruct its audiences as to the psychological reasons which impelled young men to take drugs, as to the likelihood of further and more serious racial riots, and as to troubles if not outright mutinies in the

American army. Also, about the ingenious but basically easy ways in which revolutionaries could cripple any major city. Unlike the burgeoning "underground" or the New Left press and magazines, the respectable ones did not gloat over such frightening realities and possibilities. They were being presented with "we-don't-like-it-any-more-than-you-do-but-we-must-face-it" air. The average citizen was soon made to feel it was unsophisticated to be shocked or even annoyed at such revelations and vistas. This half-orgiastic and half-cataclysmic vision of contemporary life was being offered for his instruction and soon for his amusement. Until recently there used to be a clear-cut separation between things which we were supposed to be worried about and things which were supposed to entertain us. But now, as one look at an average day's television programs will show, this distinction has been fairly obliterated.

SUCH REFLECTIONS must not be allowed to distract us from our subject—youth and the university. The flame of protest already burned brightly in 1966-67. Partly, of course, it was the escalating Vietnam war which was responsible. But also, and above all, it became clear that dissent pays. Not merely or mainly in the crude sense of the expression but in terms of public attention, or sometimes even from the therapeutic point of view. To the relative handful of people who have opposed America's over-commitment in Southeast Asia from the start and to the even smaller circle of people who have constantly been critics of American society, there was now joined a rapidly growing body of those who found it fashionable or profitable, or both, to challenge the U.S. Government and to denounce the iniquitous social system under which we live.

The new youth culture soon became a catspaw of dissent; or, rather, the two have entered into a symbiotic relationship. Logically, there was no reason for such an association.

Presumably one could like rock music, nudity, drugs, and yet be a staunch defender of the status quo; or, in theory, strong passion against social injustice and depredations of American imperialism could be combined with a "square" appearance, distaste for pornography, and preference for cocktails as against pot. Yet very soon such eclecticism became almost unthinkable. I have already mentioned Dr. Spock as the scandalous exception which goes far to prove the rule. If one talked to the young only about politics, at least in the beginning, then they soon grew bored. If one argued for long hair and short skirts only on grounds of fashion, then one was shallow and unlikely to obtain from a sociologist or social psychologist that certificate of deep social significance so necessary for successful merchandising of the product in question. Separately, dissent and youth culture had been like two rivulets, barely noticeable on the American landscape. Joined, they became a mighty stream. To be sure, not quite as mighty as our journalistic and sociologist friends have often tried to persuade us. For individualism, healthy scepticism, and a sense of humor have not vanished from the land, not even among the young. But the havoc has been great.

The fusion has not always been well synchronized. Sometimes one had the impression that the youth culture set off in pursuit of dissent, sometimes vice versa. The Beatles, if one recalls correctly, began nonpolitically, and then wisely, from their point of view, became symbolic of the anguish of post-industrial society. And within one's own university one may easily observe how the need to strike a blow against the Establishment led some middle-aged, even elderly, professors to let their hair grow, discard ties, sport beards. To be radical *and* clean-shaven is to incur automatically the suspicion of being a Maoist, or what is worse, an orthodox Communist.*

*After lengthy deliberation the Communist Party of the United States has evidently decided to do something about its "square" image.

The American university became, inevitably, the place where the fusion took place: I have mentioned before how formidable it appeared and yet how poorly defended were its approaches—a fatal combination. We have also seen in the case of the sexual revolution how absolutely trite and trivial news items, when emanating from one of what are known as prestigious universities, tended to attract national attention and then acquire vast social significance. The sequence of events was reminiscent of a chain reaction. A *small* group of students might become inspired by a random idea thrown out in a lecture or discovered in a hitherto obscure book, and proceed to do something unusual. Since the university was now news, this would find its way, as it would not have years before, to the papers. The news in turn would become the subject of investigation among social scientists, research funds would be appropriated for the study of the phenomenon in depth, etc. It then became a circular flow: the classroom—students—news—classroom—students. An enterprising social scientist might decry the "lack of relevance" of contemporary education to modern life. Sometime later, when the cry would be echoing through the campuses of the nation, he would pioneer a study of *students* demanding "relevance." At that point, as a recognized expert on the subject, he might be called upon to prescribe a program of reforms, a new and relevant curriculum, perhaps to advise the government at one or another level. And in due time, back in the classroom at a seminar, he would be analyzing why the reforms had failed, how the sources of youth's discontent went beyond the mere issue of "relevance," how much wider and more "basic" reforms must be. We have a partial but still disturbing analogy with totalitarian society. How do the rulers of the U.S.S.R., *i.e.*, its chief bureaucrats, spend most of their time? Why, by denouncing evils of bureaucracy. Just as others lust after power and material gain so there are those who have a strong need to watch over, exhort, and censor their fellow human beings.* Under certain conditions and in certain professions, *e.g.*, the religious ones, this quality is appropriate and valuable. But it is inappropriate and bound to bring nefarious results, as our sad times bear witness, if it is widely found among bureaucrats, professors, and editorial writers.

For an institution like the university, minding one's own business is not only a desirable precept but a *necessary* condition of its successful functioning and discharging of its obligations to society as well as its members. And the failure to abide by this maxim has been precisely the principal cause of the university's troubles and will, if it persists, lead to its downfall. There is at the moment a great tendency to congratulate ourselves on the evident slackening of student troubles, on the apparent weakening of student radicalism. But these have not been causes but only the most eye-catching symptoms of the crisis. Whether they recur or not, the crisis will continue until its real causes are appreciated and remedied, and the university restored to its proper role as the place of learning.

These general reflections may be best illustrated by referring to one's own particular experience within a particular university. In the fall of 1969 I sat in a meeting of the faculty of arts and sciences at Harvard listening to a speaker urging that the faculty declare itself on something or other, anyway a political question on which, until a short time before, nobody, whether Communist or conservative, would have assumed the faculty, as a *body,* had any business declaring itself in one sense or another. This time, urged the speaker, *History* itself demanded that we "take a stand" (*i.e.*, vote for his resolution). Nobody laughed, though many in the

---

*As Cromwell remarked in 1655 about some of his fellow Puritan revolutionaries, "Is there not yet a strange itch upon the spirits of men? Nothing will satisfy them unless they can press their finger upon their brethren's conscience to pinch them there . . . ."

audience would have decried such oratory as pretentious if not preposterous had it come from a national figure. When did this era of bombast start? In 1966, even though we were aware of the forces encroaching upon the university which I have been describing, we (meaning most persons I knew in and about the university) were fairly confident that the essential structure of the university would emerge un-damaged. Reasons for this foolish (as it was to turn out) optimism varied. There was a school of "this-simply-cannot-happen-here"; Harvard was not Berkeley. There was another group which based its confidence on less invidious and more structural reasons. Harvard, through its Houses and its tutorial system, which brought most of its students into close association with at least one faculty member, avoided that impersonality and educational factory atmosphere which characterized so many large schools. There was, finally, the over-rational approach which I shared: yes, there were all sorts of danger signs and disquieting trends . . . But when all has been said and Harvard's now somewhat differently viewed involvement in the Washington picture accounted for, the fact remained that most people, faculty and students alike, were busy and appeared to enjoy what they were doing.

The setting of the first incident—it was to shake our confidence somewhat—was appropriate insofar as it demon-strated the confluence of those forces which, some of them unwittingly, were to plunge the university into deep trouble. This was the so-called McNamara episode.

Sometime before, there had been set up at Harvard the Institute of Politics. Its avowed purpose was to conduct research on various issues connected with public policy and also, if not principally, to arouse the undergraduates' interest in public affairs. (That we should have such worries, a sorely-tried college administrator would exclaim today.) But in 1965-66 we, or rather *they (i.e.,* people who worry about

what the students do or don't worry about), still believed
they had to combat "Apathy." To counteract it, it was
thought best to have select groups of undergraduates,
shepherded by faculty members of the Institute, encounter
some high officials who would impart to them the challenge,
responsibilities, and allurements of power and influence. And
it was in pursuance of that plan that the then Secretary of
Defense appeared in Cambridge, Mass. to inaugurate the
much-heralded program; to mix and mingle and impart tales
of high policy to the presumably eager and appreciative small
groups of the young. But this was 1966. The dynamic and
likeable Secretary, who would have been greeted with
curiosity and courtesy two years before, had become
identified in the mind of some undergraduates with the
machine which was only awaiting their graduation to snatch
them and make them do things they did not want to do,
possibly in Southeast Asia.

The local radical group decided that the visit was a unique
opportunity for what was to become known as a "confrontation." And so it came to pass. After the scheduled discussion
with a small and intimate group of students, the Secretary
was faced by an unscheduled demonstration, his car
surrounded and he himself invited to discuss national policies
under rather ominous conditions. The Secretary was finally
allowed to proceed. But not before he made a statement to
his besiegers. He recalled that he had been a student himself.
But he was then both more polite and tougher than they.

The last part of that statement deserves a digression. It
soon became obvious that an important undercurrent of the
university revolt was the drive to destroy the myth of the
self-possessed men which has played such an important role
in the structure of authority in this country and perhaps even
more so in England. This tradition had many embodiments.
There was the British district officer on the Northwest
Frontier unflinchingly confronting a crowd of unruly

tribesmen and through his sheer moral superiority making them back down. There was the pre-Depression business tycoon, unruffled by protests and imprecations of the reformers, supremely confident that by amassing wealth he was conferring benefits on society. The latest link in this tradition of unflappable men with iron nerves, and hence a prime target for anguished students and professors, was precisely the high administration official and/or the college president. Always self-possessed, always able to blunt the edge of an emotional protest or attack with a timely story or joke, which would make assaulters or protesters feel ridiculously overanxious, this individual stood squarely in the path of advancing dissent. And until he was made to plead, engage in a dialogue, promise to reform—in brief, was broken—the Establishment would not be seriously damaged. Sometime later it was perceived that the most effective way of breaking down this self-confidence was not through physical intimidation. But people unmoved by physical threats would sometimes cringe at, or at least become flustered if lashed with obscene language. Then when the famous dialogue began, visual terror supplemented the verbal one: how could a normally accoutered college administrator hold his own in a debate with a long-haired youngster arrayed in the uniform of dissent?

The McNamara episode was, then, a grave portent. Participants in the disturbance were let off with a warning that any future behavior of that sort would have serious consequences. It is easy but somewhat unfair to criticize that decision of Harvard's administration. How can one second-guess people's decisions when confronted with a situation they have not faced before? But it is reasonable to inquire whether the attitude displayed on that occasion was realistic or not. In the case of a somewhat larger crisis, Neville Chamberlain perhaps had no viable alternative but to capitulate to Adolf Hitler. But how fatuous of him to declare upon his return from Munich that he brought "peace in our time." And so in the case of our incident. One cannot be sure that suspensions or expulsions would have produced desirable results. But there was every reason to take a hard look at what was becoming known as student activism and at how much of it was compatible with the functioning of the university. At the time quite a number of students signed a statement of regret and apology to the Secretary of Defense. Those represented clearly a majority sentiment among the undergraduate body. But, in future developments, representatives of the majority would go on signing statements while the minority went on precipitating incidents. This led those delegated to deal with such matters to pay increasing heed to views and demands of the minority.

The legend was pricked. The old model of the man in authority, kind but firm, never at a loss for a light joke or a tough-minded decision, now faded from the campus and (naturally in view of the now symbiotic relationship between the world of the university and that of politics) began to recede on the national scene. He was succeeded by the *negotiator.* The latter was sure that if they only all sat down together and discussed the whole problem, they would arrive at a mutually acceptable solution. It was symptomatic that in the wake of the McNamara episode the "format," as it is called, of visits by high public officials was altered. Before the next potentate, Mr. Arthur Goldberg, then U.S. Ambassador to the United Nations, was to grace the campus with his presence, some discreet sounding took place as to under what conditions dissenting youth would forgo stirring up trouble. The idea of notables coming to have an off-the-record discussion with a select few had to be jettisoned. A public official could purchase his right to appear on the campus by engaging in a public debate with a representative of dissent. Since such debates grew increasingly acrimonious, famous men in office grew increasingly disinclined to come. Very soon the idea of the U.S. Secretary of State appearing on a campus of a leading university became as incongruous as that of an official of the Communist party in, say, 1953 or 1957. To be sure, famous men who had left office would still come to let the audience in on reasons which made them see the light, the errors of President Johnson's policies, and the need for peaceful dissent.

The year 1967 brought another development which, I think, was crucial to the so-called revolt of the young, but which somehow had not attracted much attention from the chroniclers of the phenomenon. It was revealed how the C.I.A. had funnelled funds into some organizations and foundations dealing with cultural and educational activities, among them something called the National Student Association, an organization of whose existence relatively few students at Harvard were aware, and those who were (except for its officials) did not care. The background of the story was a typical American tragedy or rather tragi-comedy.

Following World War II the United States found itself in—well, anyway, call it a world-wide competition with the Soviet Union. The arts, literature, youth festivals, and the like became arenas for this struggle, and who could complain as long as our competition was mostly confined to those fields. But such activities required money. The USSR had a ready phalanx of foreign Communists, of its own artists and youth organizations. As against it, how could the U.S. extol the artistic and esthetic side of the "American Way of Life" among European intellectuals, the Asian non-Communist left, and African nationalists? The sensible way to deal with the problem would have been in a entirely above-board way: through an organization on the model of the British Council. But the word "propaganda" still had a jarring sound to American ears and certainly to members of the Congress. There was a further complication. Foreigners, and among them especially intellectuals, and even more especially those of a radical even if non-Communist persuasion, were viewed with the darkest suspicion by congressional chairmen. Yet it was desirable, and not only from the propaganda point of view, that the voice of the non-Communist left in Europe and Asia should be encouraged, provided with a forum in the form of magazines, conferences, and so on. It would have been hopeless to expect that any "open" U.S. agency should be allowed to subsidize that entirely unsinister activity. Or that in that era sufficient numbers of young Americans would find time, inclination, and resources to tilt at foreign conferences with the representatives of Soviet youth.* There was, to be sure, the U.S. Information Service, but to many on Capitol Hill even its routine activities smacked of subversion. Who does not recall the famous raid conducted on its overseas libraries by Messrs. Cohn and Schine on behalf of Senator McCarthy? In brief, there was only one American government agency which could safely and efficiently subsidize the above activities: the C.I.A., for spying, unlike cultural propaganda, became fairly respectable following World War II.

But, in 1967, to almost everybody's shock, the whole story came out in the open. Those esoteric magazines filled with articles on existentialism and Marxism, that conference in Bamako where sociologists from the West and the Third World held that memorable dialogue, those American students upholding the reputation of their country at an International Youth Festival and succeeding in having a resolution condemning American imperialism pass only by a small majority, they were all now (in Soviet parlance) "unmasked" and revealed as tools of Allen Dulles! It was in vain that all those organizations now renounced their

---

*As to the character of the Soviet youth organization, it is sufficient to recall that its two successive heads passed directly from that office to head the secret police.

government links and announced that from then on they would take money only from American foundations, that internationally famous poets and literary critics protested ignorance as to the ultimate source of fees for their articles, condemning impartially both the U.S. and Russia. The damage was done.

The young have a great capacity for suspicion. We still talk about child-like faith but never about adolescent-like trust. The story about the C.I.A. and the spider-like web it wove around various cultural and educational causes was one of the most effective catalysts of that suspicion. The government of the U.S. was *manipulating* things; it was *using* youth organizations. Those two words soon became key ones in the litany of student dissent. And their popularity augured ill for the possibility that the new authority type, the negotiator, of whom we just spoke, would be able to set things right either in the country or the university. Wasn't the whole technique of student-administration conferences a subtle effort to "manipulate" the radicals? And those little student-run seminar groups and courses (many of them with quite a radical content), which various university institutes with links to the government now offered as a gesture of appeasement to dissent, weren't they pursuing the goal of *co-opting?* The still small minority of students which was increasingly giving tone to student life at a place like Harvard was living in an atmosphere not so much of radicalism as of growing morbid suspicion and tension. Suspicion was attached not only to the U.S. government, which through its ineptitude rather than any dark designs gave the impression of deep Machiavellian deviousness. It gradually extended to many college officials, and to professors with current or previous links with Washington.

But it is unlikely that simple, politically originated suspiciousness would have had such widespread impact either within the university or the country. The latter withstood, and within a few years cast aside, somewhat similar wave of hysteria during the McCarthy period. Cults of great suspicion, whether embodied in the John Birch Society or in what might be called "liberal McCarthyism" as displayed in some left-wing periodicals, were matters of curiosity rather than consequence. Few were ready to believe that General Eisenhower had been a tool of the Communist conspiracy, or that the whole course of America's foreign policy had been predetermined by the fact that Mr. John Foster Dulles' law firm had many, many years before represented a German chemical concern.

But to political suspiciousness was joined what might be called a cosmic one. *Everybody* was trying to use the young—or so proclaimed many social scientists and the more alert journalists who in fact were demonstrating the *partial* truth of their thesis. The attitude of despair became fashionable and profitable. The Beatles had conquered America a few years before because, allegedly, they radiated innocence and romantic merriment. Now their very appearance as well as their songs bespoke the age of anxiety and despair. Gloom has swept other media of (or so it used to be known) entertainment. Serious thinkers then interpreted this as a reflection of the mood of the young and found it rather encouraging. This generation, unlike any preceding one, was not foolishly optimistic; look where such optimism had gotten the preceding generations! Optimism, in the more sophisticated journalistic and academic circles, was in 1967 already considered to be in seriously bad taste. From facing the issues squarely, which was the fashion a year or so before, the advanced view shifted to what might be called constructive pessimism: things were bad, they were bound to become worse unless and until they became perfect. The young were much praised for discovering that truth. A distinguished scientist was to attribute the students' discontent to their justified suspicion that the current generation had "no future." It was no longer the relatively simple matter of those evil men in Washington. We lived, it was discovered, in post-industrial society. If nuclear war was not going to get us, then pollution and overpopulation surely would.

This message of universal suspiciousness and gloom was bound to have some eager listeners and adherents among the people of college age. It fitted and enhanced what is probably the natural mood at a certain phase of development. It put an elegant philosophical gloss on one's personal anxieties as well as those arising out of Vietnam and national prosperity. But, by the same token, this mood, when stimulated and encouraged from the outside, was bound to turn to active wrath and seek convenient targets. A Russian poet epitomized one element of youth's longing when he exclaimed: "Life is grim and aimless, and there is no one around whose hand one might clasp." This romantic *cri de coeur* was subsequently parodied by changing the second part to " . . . there is no one around whose face one might push in." Parody or not, this was not an inconsiderable insight.

By now (1967) one was likely to become worried and depressed if one took a hard look at the American university. One could no longer be sure that as an institution it was doing much good for its students or for society at large. There was the fact that a great majority of teachers and students went about their business as before and that useful and necessary research and teaching continued. But it was doubtful that the total sum of influence the university exerted could be described as education. Students still received excellent *training,* in most cases better than that of their predecessors ten or twenty years ago. But could one also say that in the process of becoming physicists, sociologists, or classicists they had enlarged their minds as well as filling them with knowledge? That if they discarded inherited or conventional beliefs they acquired, in their place, a more dispassionate, broader outlook, rather than new stereotypes at once more rigid and vacuous? In many cases one could not. And if a great majority of students managed to preserve and develop their sense of proportion and humor while in college or graduate school, could one honestly and firmly say it was because of the university rather than despite the influences to which it subjected them?

Such gloomy reflections found a focus in the now definite pattern of incidents which was afflicting the campus. The fall of 1967 witnessed the Dow episode. Here was an escalation of the techniques employed in the McNamara case; the person was detained for several hours rather than a few minutes, and he was a recruiter for an industrial firm rather than a director of America's military machine. The gentleman in question was prevented from leaving a room where he was supposed to conduct interviews with students interested in obtaining jobs with his firm, which was accused of producing napalm bombs used by American armed forces in Vietnam. He forebore from calling upon the police to free him, and thus what was becoming famous as "confrontation" was avoided at Harvard for another year-and-a-half.

A student of revolutions should be grateful, I suppose, to study at first hand a similar development in his own time and environment. What was going to unfold at the American campuses was what might now be called a series of mini-revolutions. The Dow incident was a true prelude to a revolutionary sequence, for the reaction to it lay half-way between a rational appraisal of what happened and that atmosphere compounded of hysteria, fear, and elation which is a necessary component of a true revolution and which was to be so notable in the spring of 1969. From a formal point of view the incident was an illegal detention of an individual (and it was not clear whether this had been planned or whether the students who had been picketing the interviewer were suddenly seized by an uncontrollable urge to push their protest one step further). As such, it would have led under normal conditions to suspension and expulsion if not, indeed, criminal action against the culprits. But precisely these were not normal conditions, argued those among the faculty who condoned or "understood" the action. Students were overwrought over Vietnam; the Dow Company *did* produce napalm.

Various administrators present on the scene identified the blockaders and collected their bursar's (*i.e.,* identity) cards. But many students not directly involved turned their cards in voluntarily as a gesture of solidarity with what was described as an anti-war protest. Then arose the problem of punishment, if any. After the McNamara episode the college authorities warned that a repetition of the incident would bring most serious consequences, by which, one assumes, was meant penalties. Well, to be brief about it, the consequences of this episode were to be most serious, but as to the penalties there were to be none. The board charged with disciplinary matters concerning students became perplexed, if indeed boards can become so. Its members had dealt traditionally with problems like what to do with a student caught plagiarizing, having a girl in his room after hours, etc. Here was a problem of quite a different character involving a group rather than individuals. The board turned the matter over to the faculty as a whole, and the latter body let the offenders off with something which amounted at most to a reprimand and a warning. Even this was considered excessive by some faculty members and students: wasn't the university becoming repressive and trying to stifle legitimate political protest? We were already on the threshold of the era of sophistry, and an act which would have been unthinkable a year or two before could be excused or mitigated on several grounds: the man had been detained but he was not physically molested; he was let go after several hours; in the calculus of outrage what was the action of a few courageous students against one individual compared with what the U.S.

was doing in Vietnam? There were also arguments of a prudential nature: how would the mass of undergraduates react if the culprits were suspended or dismissed from the university? Wasn't it wise to isolate the extremists, make them realize that violence (if it was violence) was counter-productive? Or, in the opposite sense, wasn't the university administration, if not guilty, then insensitive by allowing such *provocative* visits to the campus? And if so, wasn't the students' action in fact productive because it taught the university a lesson? Can you punish people for misguided idealism? Is it misguided idealism when students instead of just talking about the war *do* something about it?

The Dow episode stands, then, as a watershed in the history of our mini-revolution. At each subsequent outrage the small group of believers in exemplary severity would sigh and say: "Had we only done something at the time of the Dow incident!" But they would be countered by an equally numerous school of the warning bell which was not heeded: the university, they claimed, missed an opportunity to engage in a real dialogue with the concerned students.

But the last opinion is not quite fair. The university did change following the incident: it became solicitous and agitated. To show that an institution can become so, let me take the example of the Faculty of Arts and Sciences, *i.e.,* the central faculty of Harvard responsible for the instruction of all undergraduates and the largest number of graduate students. Of six hundred or so members of this body, relatively few (about one hundred) used to attend its monthly meetings. These were held in a large room in University Hall, soon to become a battleground. The sessions were decorous and rather sedate affairs. Participants, after fortifying themselves with tea, proceeded to discuss various educational problems, usually of a routine nature and never longer than for two hours. In the fall of 1967 this format began to be altered. The room was inadequate to accommodate the now usually large rank of faculty members who would be summoned following the latest crisis. The rather excessive number of portraits of former presidents and deans who gaze from its walls also conveys the air of academic detachment and severity which has made it rather inappropriate for the at times somber discussion of pressing issues, though by the same token the faculty room was to serve (in the spring of 1969) as an evidently satisfactory surrogate for the Bastille or the Winter Palace. Faculty assemblies have tended to migrate to large and drafty lecture halls. Tea was dispensed with. Oratory was to grow passionate and was to become, at times, not devoid of political and even personal acrimony.

So much for agitation. On the side of solicitude, the crisis brought out the fact that a number of professors viewed themselves as special friends, advocates, and defenders of the students' cause. They did not imply in the slightest that the rest of their colleagues were not friendly; but they believed that they were more so, and took pains to advertise this belief and the complementary one that they enjoyed special trust and following among the recipients of their affection. The university administration, for its part, was persuaded to give a tangible expression to this concern for the students' needs and wants. The result was a joint faculty-student committee partly elected, partly appointed by the dean. And as it happens in such cases and on such occasions, the people who found themselves on this committee were for the most part those who had originated the idea. It was never exactly clear what this faculty-student committee was supposed to do. But it was hoped that it would usher in a new era of communication between those two hitherto separate bodies, the faculty and the undergraduates.

Laudable though the motives of all concerned probably were, the idea had a basic flaw. It proceeded from the hugely erroneous notion that the university consists of several distinct interest groups, that the expressions "students" and "faculty" are in any sense analogous to employees and employers. It was desirable, of course, to have *some* institutionalized means of gauging students' sentiment on various problems touching the university, and a representative student body would have been very desirable (student government at Harvard had for long been moribund and of little interest to the bulk of undergraduates). But the hastily constructed council, with undefined powers, tended to produce the impression that there was something on the order of "studentdom" just as there is "the working class." This was, then, a false idea whose time had come. Even the most doctrinaire Marxist will now admit that there is a vast difference in status, income, and feeling between, say, a highly-skilled worker and a ditch-digger. But otherwise sensible people would soon say that the students (or as it was sometimes repulsively phrased, "the kids") wanted this-or-that. And then rhetoric would soar. People would unblushingly proclaim that the American students are an "exploited class," an expression which presumably was to conjure up visions of a nineteenth-century English or French proletarian, today's denizen of a Calcutta slum, or a sharecropper in Mississippi. As such the whole notion ceased to be ridiculous, and in a way became tragic if not indeed obscene. It was only a bit less so when the facilities and opportunities before an American college student were compared with those of his European contemporary, or his freedom with that of a Russian or Pole. And in due time, and in a perverse sense, the notion was to become true: the American student is being exploited by middle-aged men who for their own purpose or profit propagandize him to become agitated and disturbed and to abandon that gaiety and ambition so appropriate to his age and so necessary to social progress.

The faculty-student committee was to become unwittingly a catalyst in a deepening crisis. It provided a forum for oratory, some good, some bad; some calling for bold new action, some calling for prudence or restraint. But since the committee had no legislative power, the resolutions which it passed could have effect only if accepted or carried through by the appropriate faculty or administrative body, which was bound to lead to some confusion. Or if resolutions had no effect, this indicated, of course, the insensitivity of the university to the demands of its constituencies. That, in turn, fortified the impression on the part of some students and faculty that the university was a political institution. "They" (and the cast of "they" varied: the president, the deans, the conservative professors and then, finally, the Corporation who not only tyrannized over the faculty but represented the American Establishment, capitalism or what-have-you) had power, and "they" jealously guarded it against legitimate claims of democracy.

One could see then—and a similar process was taking place on other American campuses—a growing indoctrination in unrealism and the burgeoning of masochistic myths. The college was no longer a place where one spent four years (happily or otherwise, but anyway just four years), but the place where there were forged the chains of conformity which one would have to bear for the rest of one's life. The president was no longer a man who delivered appropriate speeches upon appropriate occasions, stuffy or friendly, popular or otherwise, but anyway a man of whom one was barely aware as one went about one's studies and amusements; he was an essential cog in the system of oppression which stretched from one's home to the White House. Those college officials, solicitous in a kindly or busybody way, were now petty agents of repression. One could not even be sure about this professor of physics or that professor of English. Seemingly engrossed in his work, wasn't he in fact cheating or betraying his students by excessively engaging in research, advising the government, remaining indifferent to Vietnam and racial equality, unmindful of the anguish and legitimate claims of the young?

Someone wrote about the outbreak of World War I that it offered the melancholy spectacle of middle-aged men urging the young to go out and fight. The same could be said about the now fairly widespread disorders which afflicted American universities in 1968. What was, in fact, a spreading mass neurosis was hailed as healthy student activism by some within the university, and by more outside it, by politicians, newspapers, magazines and other media. Many praised and encouraged the mood because of a combination of conviction and ignorance, because of the belief that the folly of Vietnam could be arrested through it, or that it would lead to beneficial results on the racial and economic fronts. But many were less than sincere in their advocacy, or (as was more common) in seeing some positive sides to the depressing and wasteful affliction which was now affecting many young men. A very prominent national politician was sure in a private conversation that by now (it was spring 1969) everybody, himself included, was "sick and tired of student disorders." But in his public utterances he continued to praise the "spirit of protest" among the young. A distinguished psychiatrist discoursed, again in private, on the pathological aspects of the so-called activism; yet in his articles and talks re-proclaimed the current student generation as unique and praiseworthy in its spirit of altruism.

It was, thus, understandable that university administrations and faculties bowed increasingly to the mood or, rather, the relentless propaganda which urged them to pay homage to the idealism of the youth and to accommodate themselves to the new spirit. There began something of a competition among the more alert college officials to try to anticipate what students (*i.e.,* any student group of critical mass) might conceivably demand in the future, and to grant it before such a demand could be formulated or even conceived. One might have thought that, even though analogies from politics ill apply to the university, the university officials would have recourse to ascertaining what in fact was the majority opinion of students on various issues and demands. But majorities, as revolutionaries have always known, tend to be conservative. To submit a crucial demand to a scrupulously conducted student referendum would only have served to infuriate the radical minority, and prudent administrators eschewed such stratagems. On the other hand, a university deemed itself fortunate which had on its faculty or staff a popular but not unreasonable radical, *i.e.*, one whose violent denunciation of the U.S. government and questioning of the American way of life (in 1968 this was still enough for the purpose) would earn him trust and a following among the students, and who could thus deflect their wrath from their own institution.

I do not want to convey the impression that the college students were merely being manipulated by outside and inside agitators and public relations men in different guises. But those who refused to be so went on in their individualistic way being students and, thus, could not form a countervailing force to those bent upon transforming the campus into a Living Theatre. It was incorrect to say that the campus was being "politicized." Activism was in fact a negation of politics, for it consisted in substituting a highly ritualistic type of behavior for political argument and action.

A vivid proof of this was provided by the behavior of those young dissenters who flung themselves into the campaign on behalf of Senator Eugene McCarthy. Young men and women who wanted to solicit votes for their idol were told to trim their hair, shave their beards, shed their beads, and lengthen their skirts. But one could not help reflecting that if the primary and overwhelming objectives of the virtuous youth were political, and if the average voter did have a revulsion against the new styles (which is at least debatable when it comes to the mini-skirt) then that sacrifice on the altar of conformity should have been made permanent rather than just for the purposes of a primary campaign in New Hampshire. Wasn't the achievement of peace and social justice worth a crew-cut and knee-length skirt? The McCarthy campaign illustrated the startling lesson that the place for students interested in politics is, as for everyone else, in politics. But later on even this tautology could not withstand the new logic which is a much more characteristic phenomenon of our times then that of the New Left. So the students *did* try to work "within the system," and what did it get them? Did the system reciprocate this touching restraint and faith? How square of the proverbial American boy to take his bat and ball and go home when the game goes against him! Ought he not to consider bashing the umpire on the head and beaning his opponent?

THEN CAME THE UNHAPPY SPRING and summer of 1968. The French student revolt heartened those sociologists who had maintained all along that student unrest was a world-wide phenomenon. It was also and even more vividly demonstrated how universal is the breed of climbers on the bandwagon, and how in their eagerness to get on one they often stumble and are left behind. While General De Gaulle hesitated and tottered, though always in his majestic manner, there were many voices proclaiming that he, the Fifth Republic, and capitalism in France, were finished and that youth had shown the way to the new glorious age of participatory democracy. This was the gist of an ecstatic article in the *New Republic* by M. Jean-Jacques Servan-Schreiber. But then the General recovered and the students dispersed. De Gaulle was eventually to go, but his successor was to be neither Sartre nor Cohn-Bendit, but the epitome of the bourgeois style, M. Georges Pompidou. M. Servan-Schreiber went back to work within the (French) system and to enlighten the Americans on what was wrong with theirs.

The fact that Czech, American, and French students were in ferment in that spring of '68 may appear to yield validity to the "this-is-a-world-wide-phenomenon" view. But the objective circumstances of each case were vastly different. There are people who would claim that objective circumstances don't matter, that the psychological alienation of the American undergraduate is as much a justification for revolt as the very palpable lack of freedom of the student in Prague. But, if you believe that, you will believe anything, which has precisely been our problem in America.

The 1968 events at Columbia demonstrated that the American university was now ripe for a frontal assault. It was possible to examine the events with a view to various lessons. The police should not have been called; or they should have been called sooner. The university should have handled various sensitive issues differently, etc. But all such comments and criticisms amounted in their sum to an avowal that the American university was now so weak and had so departed from its purpose that almost anything—a political event outside, an error of judgment on the part of an administrator, a whim of some extraneous group—could plunge the whole institution into a state of mass hysteria. In time this condition would pass or would become ameliorated. But we do not call a man sane if he has *intermittent* attacks of madness and spends the intervals in worrying about whether and when the next one is coming. And in such a case one wonders whether the cure is advanced by helpful acquaintances offering the opinion that in this mad world it is no wonder that one becomes unhinged; that there must be hidden guilt feeling which causes those attacks. A university can function and be useful under the most hazardous circumstances. A clandestine Polish university went on functioning in German-occupied Warsaw during World War II, even though its faculty and students risked a concentration camp or worse if their enterprise was discovered by the Gestapo. It was a real university because its members believed that despite (and because of) the horrors which went on outside, it was important for them to teach and to learn. But this was not the message which was being imparted to young Americans in that spring of 1968, nor for some time afterwards.

As Harvard reassembled in the autumn, the feeling was neatly divided between those who held that "this-can't-happen-here" and those who awaited (some with apprehension, some with hidden excitement) the moment for the other shoe to drop. On the side of "this-can't-happen" were the arguments that the situation here was entirely unlike that at Columbia: there the faculty was quite distant from the undergraduates, the tutorial system here assured a close contact, minimized alienation. Harvard had the house system, *i.e.,* the university was not as centralized and impersonal as most other large schools, etc. Pessimists, on the other hand, pointed out the unhappy augury: the 1968 commencement had been interrupted by rain and the exercises had to be moved indoors for the first time in about thirty years. Radical student organizations flourished at Harvard as much as at Columbia, if not more so. What the movies, television and current literature were prescribing as the proper setting for youth culture was becoming increasingly characteristic of Harvard Square. The change in the appearance of students and of persons around the university had come very precipitously. A friend bewailed the attrition of the traditional well-kempt and neatly-dressed Harvard undergraduate. (It was characteristic that many people were more affected and afflicted by the change in the external rather than essential characteristics of the university.) I tried to console him by pointing out that drastic and unpredictable change was the rule in this society. One day soon he will be crossing the Square and there, among the men of long hair, dingily dressed, there will be a ghost of the past, a boy with a crew-cut, seersucker jacket, and gray flannel trousers. He would dismiss him as an optical illusion, but the next day he will see two of them, then three, and then a great mass of seersucker-jacketed and flannel-trousered young men would burst out all over the landscape sweeping everything else aside. No, not in his time, my friend kept insisting. For anybody who believes the motto of Winchester College that "manners makyth man" this was an especially unhappy time. unhappy time.

There were some academics who looked around to see what other universities were doing to ward off an onslaught *à la* Columbia. That in itself was significant. Before there had been considerable self-confidence on the part of the leading American universities, in which their faculties, students and trustees shared; *they* could cope with their own problems and did not have to pay attention to what was being done at *X* or *Y* university. Now this institutional individualism (or, if one prefers, arrogance) was breaking down. No university was an island. Those who had ignored the existence of such institutions now watched anxiously for the news from Southern Illinois or the latest bulletin from San Francisco State College.

The whole picture could hardly provide much consolation or instruction as to how to circumvent trouble. To paraphrase Tolstoy again, every threatened university appeared to react in a different but usually unfortunate manner. Here was the president of one, who was spending all his waking hours "mixing" with the students. He would be held up as a model for emulation precisely at the point when, on the verge of a nervous and physical breakdown, the poor man announced that he was quitting. There was another educational leader being much praised for another technique of earning the youth's trust: he was ceaselessly denouncing the Establishment and eulogizing the idealism of the "now generation." But the danger was that the students would get used to being praised, while the alumni might not to being denounced. In one case the university administration dealt firmly with disrupters but then was castigated by their parents for an "overkill" in meting out punishments (an interesting simile testifying as to how things were becoming utterly and hopelessly mixed up in some people's minds). In another university the president, faculty, and students solemnly called upon the President of the United States to solve all the major (and some minor) problems facing America, declaring that until such time peace could not return to the nation's campuses.

The technique of blaming the government for the troubles besetting the university appeared to have some advantages, as well as an element of validity. In fact, it made the university more vulnerable to the radical's rebuttal. If the U.S. government was wicked, why does the university continue to collaborate with it? How could it claim that it was neutral in the struggle between the Establishment and dissent if it retained Professor X who advised the Pentagon, if it harbored research projects designed to develop the economies of some Asian countries and thereby preserve them from Communism? Was that neutrality? The university's subsequent plea that it favored social change, (why, even a peaceful revolution!) was met by a self-proclaimed radical with derision. Did not the bulk of courses in the social sciences endorse implicitly or explicitly the two-party system, free enterprise, etc.—in other words capitalism—and hence imperialism? How many teachers discoursed on the legitimacy of revolution, the evils of American imperialism, the various aspects and techniques of liberation? A hard-pressed administrator might be able to name a few individuals and courses. Sheer "tokenism," the radical would conclude triumphantly. In brief, whatever you did, whether you were soft or hard, whether you believed in students or did not, you had to face, as (in the fall of 1968) you surveyed the American educational front, the stark reality. Everywhere there were issues—they would lead to demands—demands would bring about incidents. You might put a cheerful interpretation upon them and call them *isolated* incidents; but, even so, unless you were terribly lucky, incidents would lead to a crisis.

At Harvard that fall one could still congratulate oneself cautiously that portents of major disaster were still absent. Some of my colleagues abandoned the line of argument that Harvard would escape because it was "different" but still held to a cautious hope that it might avoid a Columbia-like disturbance. The main thing was (argued those prudent and sensible people) to wait out the present storm, not to confront any issues sharply, but to make timely concessions. Eventually the mood of the students was bound to change, the university would return to its normal pace. In brief, don't rock the boat because it is already listing and some people are trying to pull out the plugs. . . .

The trouble with that argument was that it again compared academic life with politics or with labor relations. The art of negotiations and of compromise is a useful and necessary one in politics. There you resolve, or alleviate, a conflict through elections or political deals. But you cannot determine the validity of a mathematical or biological theory by taking a vote; and though this fact is not as immediately obvious, the same truth obtains in history or economics. An institution which, though impeccably rigorous in other respects, decides to establish a department of astrology certainly could not be called a university. In other words, the university may not seek a compromise with, or grant concessions to, nonsense, no matter how popular. And almost equally debilitating would be to allow anything, whether it be religion, politics, or sports to get in the way of its main purpose. These truths which almost everybody, students and faculty alike, would have held to be self-evident around 1955, and which were becoming convincing to American society at large, were no longer so in 1968. The university's function, it was held in certain circles, was to satisfy a wide variety of wants and needs: some religious, some ideological or political in their nature. By trying to be reasonable about unreasonable demands, the university was yielding an appearance of legitimacy to any and all claims upon it. One recalls again how in the early 1960s the U.S. Ambassador to Japan was stabbed and the would-be assassin declared that his act was in protest against the insensitivity of the American and Japanese governments to the plight of near-sighted people. Greater power and/or liberation of the near-sighted would not have been the most unreasonable demand advanced upon Harvard University in 1968-69.

In fact, one reflects that Harvard along with some other schools was probably saved from a worse fate by the very multiplicity and diversity of demands advanced upon them that dismal year. The so-called issues would get in the way of each other. In the process of attacking the university, various groups would suddenly be seized by splits and doubts as to whether they were fighting to destroy or to restructure this bastion of the Establishment. At the very height of the spring 1969 crisis, one group proclaimed that its goal was "to make it impossible for the school to go on." But then, when it was rumored that the Harvard Corporation was contemplating closing the university, one of those mass meetings comprising both rebels and so-called moderates shouted a unanimous approval of the resolution affirming that the Corporation had no right to shut down *their* university. It was possible to work oneself into a highly emotional state by believing that Harvard was one of the main forces behind (or, conversely, an instrument of) American imperialism, but then almost immediately one was enjoined not to neglect its role as the oppressor of Negroes, women, American Indians, and (last but by no means least) of the white middle-class youth. But then if one accepted the notion of the university as the supreme evil in American life, what reserves of outrage were left for the Pentagon or the Chase Manhattan Bank?

A true radical would have eschewed a frontal attack upon the university. From the outside it might have looked like a bastion of the Establishment; in fact it was a headquarters of dissent. At Harvard, though in a more dignified way than at some other places, the university administration had gone far in trying to conciliate—the traditionally-minded would say appease—advocates of change and reform. But as our whole analysis has indicated, such considerations play but little part when young people's passions and their elders' resentments and ambitions have been aroused, and the institutional framework of authority has broken down or been severely damaged. A famous alpinist, asked why he proposed to climb Mount Everest, replied "Because it is there." And so Harvard was there, an enticing target for some as the symbol of the political and economic establishment, for others the epitome of the academic one.

One waited for some issue to ripen to eclipse temporarily other issues, and thus to allow a group of students to work themselves into feverish excitement on this score, coupled with the faculty's paroxysm of solicitude for the "kids," enabling the whole atmosphere to escalate from one of tension to that of hysteria. This had been the scenario at Columbia—an issue, the take-over of a building, the university officials' summon to the police, real and alleged police brutalities, excitement now gripping a large proportion of the faculty and the student body, a madhouse.

A FUTURE HISTORIAN may well decide that there was a conscious plot to precipitate the trouble at Harvard in exactly the form it was to take in April 1969; but I doubt it. Rather, it appears to have been the case of a mounting excitement within the radical student group itself, and of members groping for some means to release their wrath.

Columbia suggested that taking over a building was the red cloth necessary to make the bull, *i.e.,* the university administration, charge and impale itself on general indignation. But the analogy with the bullfight breaks down insofar as the matador (the rebelling students) in this case was at times so excited as almost to charge the bull rather than vice versa, while at other times he was prudent to the point of refusing to enter the arena altogether without a guarantee that he would emerge without a scratch. Thus the attack came partly spontaneously, a product of uncontrollable excitement generated both within and outside the group which undertook it, but also as a result of calculation that a violent action would not be followed by serious punishments. And as we have seen and shall see, there were solid grounds for that supposition.

The fall of 1968 was conspicuous for the heroics of the Harvard football team, which concluded its undefeated season by snatching a tie in the very last second of its game against Yale. Perhaps that had a dampening effect on the burgeoning protest. But protest would not be dampened in the Harvard Yard. Theoretically, political or any other mass meetings and demonstrations were not allowed within the enclosure which contains most of the administrative and some lecture buildings, corresponding to what in most other American universities is the central campus. But, by now, such prohibitions (in fact the whole corpus of college rules and regulations) were in the process of "withering away," to use Karl Marx's famous phrase. One grew used to the sight of a group of students being addressed by some passionate orator with a bullhorn. Those meetings would usually take place on the steps of, or in front of, Memorial Church, cheering those clerics in and around the university who had been fearful that religion might be becoming irrelevant to the new breed of angry young men. But then almost imperceptibly the group or crowd would inch toward University

Hall, containing the faculty assembly room and the offices of many deans and administrators.* Obviously this building was becoming a target. Why University Hall, rather than Massachusetts Hall? The former was associated with the faculty (*i.e.*, professors, deans, *et al.*) while the latter represented the government of the university as a whole, those mysterious and yet assuredly sinister lawyers and businessmen who ruled Harvard on behalf of American capitalism. Precisely, some would say; the enraged student still stood in greater awe of that distant body with its sinister connections than of those solicitous and pleading deans and professors. But there was a less romantic explanation. Massachusetts Hall is small, bespeaking that understatement so characteristic of older Harvard; University Hall is commodious, with a large room for mass meetings, and many offices and bathrooms.

It was not only in those meetings in the open air, which New England's winter was soon and mercifully to curtail, that one could hear rumblings of the approaching assault. The faculty was trying anxiously to resolve several con-tentious problems before, God forbid, they could grow into "issues." One such was the question of a separate department for Afro-American studies. It was rather hurriedly voted into existence despite widespread doubts about the advisability of having a special concentration in this form as against offering relevant courses within the already existing divisions of the university. The faculty discovered (its fastidious members with some horror) that there already *was* a course, if you please, not only taught by students but by people entirely unconnected with the university. An accommodating instruc-

---

*The topography of the Yard is complemented by the vast pile of the university library, various lecture halls, freshman dormitories and its oldest building, Massachusetts Hall, housing the offices of the governing body of the University, the President and Fellows, known as the Corporation.

tor lent his course to some resourceful students who turned it into a miniature Free University. And not so miniature at that: seven hundred or so students were instructed, if that is the proper word, in thirty or so sections, in a most kaleidoscopic variety of subjects ranging from Shakespeare to the misdeeds of American imperialism and racism. The style of instruction was equally varied. In some sections one had still some relics of the traditional repressive system: assigned readings, lectures, and grades. In others, the participants decided their own grades, and their titular instructor was treated as and considered himself as (in the phrase just coming into fashion) an "educational resource" rather than an authoritarian leader. Though radically conceived and led, the course enjoyed great popularity among students of varied political persuasion, which (some would hold) reflected on the more staid methods of instruction, others on students' good judgment. But this experiment led even radically inclined members of the faculty to fear that this was but an entering wedge of something which, left unchecked, might destroy the regular method of instruction. This apprehension was neatly checked by another one: would an attempt to interfere become *the* issue? The Department of Social Relations which formally, and rather unhappily, sheltered that educational innovation, tried tentatively and cautiously to reform and/or curtail the experiment. But though the department contained specialists in sociology, human motivation and what was becoming a flourishing branch of sociology and might be called studentology, it was not making much headway in its negotiations with the managers of the enterprise.

Yet the eventual and acute trouble was to spring from another source. As sometimes happens, the manner in which the trouble arose, even if not its cause, was very largely unexpected and paradoxical. Confrontation came, you might say, out of communication. And, perhaps, this happens quite often. Do you help the cause of human understanding and eventually of friendship by forcing people of differing temperaments into a forced and frequent association with each other? This may not be so bad if people are thus associated for the purpose of *doing* something. But if you force people into frequent meetings where they just talk, supposedly to, but inevitably, after some time, *at* each other. . . .

The student-faculty committee organized in the wake of the Dow affair, as it became known, or the *SFAC*, illustrated some of the dangers inherent in communication. The hope was that such a smallish group of about thirty, associating on terms of equality, with the chairmanship rotating between the two constituencies, would enable each side to understand the other better. But mutual irritation is very often the price you pay for mutual understanding. Then, the committee did not consist of students and faculty. You had there some students and some faculty members thrown together. There were moderate students and radical students, professors who tended to be prudent when it came to the so-called "thorny" issues and professors who were bold. Unwittingly *SFAC* served to focus attention and enhance excitement on the most troublesome (and by the same token, most promising from the point of view of disruption) issues. And thus finally it stumbled upon the Issue.

This was the ROTC. To those who were disgruntled over Vietnam the ROTC was the most scandalous form of the university helping the war machine. It gave academic credits for courses in military and naval science; provided a building and other facilities for that instruction; bestowed professorial rank on military and naval officers attached to the school for that purpose. There was, on the other hand, the undeniable fact that membership in the ROTC at Harvard was, as at most other private universities, entirely voluntary. One could feel, one still can, that there is no contradiction between being most emphatically opposed to the U.S. policies in Vietnam and yet acknowledging the right of those so inclined to prepare for a commission in the armed forces while pursuing their studies. To be sure, the university in the process was giving aid and comfort to the government of the United States, something which in the eyes of some was regrettable if not reprehensible. But then, if one felt that the government was a hostile power, the logical step was to renounce any and all federal connections and funds with the exception of those in the medical field. And *that* somehow not even the most radical member of the faculty was ready to recommend.

The beauty of the ROTC issue in the eyes of many faculty members was that you need not put it so bluntly and indelicately. No, you were not punishing the Pentagon and depriving some students of the opportunity to earn commissions (as well as having their studies subsidized by the U.S. government). You were simply curtailing or excising that branch of studies which was not regulated by academic standards and by usual faculty rules. And in the process you would earn the trust, and (who knows) perhaps the gratitude of the radical students who would interpret it as the university striking out at the iniquitous government. Anyway, discussion within the *SFAC*, and then discussion within the faculty, focused more and more on the Issue. There were, as one might expect, several views within the faculty, all cogent, as to how this blow for freedom and the bid for the students' trust might be expressed. Don't give it any explicit political meaning, argued some. Just withdraw academic credits from the ROTC courses and professorial titles from its teachers. The ROTC, then, could continue to exist as an informal organization on the analogy of, say, the university choral society. No, that was not enough, argued more radical members. The ROTC had to be ejected from the campus lock, stock, and barrel. There were also ingenious proposals seeking a compromise between those two views. The discussion went on and, as it did, excitement grew among the student body. At one point a number of students occupied the premises when the faculty was to discuss this and other questions. For some reason this action was viewed as more reprehensible than the forcible detention of Secretary McNamara and of the emissary of the Dow Company. The administrative board recommended that a few students who were involved and who had participated in previous disturbances should be suspended, *i.e.,* expelled for various periods. But the faculty, which this time was allowed to meet, rejected this recommendation and suspended the suspension.

Now we reached a new plateau of the Issue. The whole sequence of events demonstrated (some of my colleagues argued) that the university administration was losing touch with our young men and women. We had to restructure the governance of the university. We no longer could afford to hold our faculty meetings without student participation, or at least attendance. (A few years before the most inquisitive undergraduate would have regarded as intolerable the notion that he should spend a few hours in the afternoon listening to a faculty debate.) The meetings of that body now grew tempestuous. It was no longer the matter of a leisurely discussion of, say, whether the Department of Biochemistry should be rebaptized to one of biological chemistry. At a meeting one orator invoked the spectre of the class struggle within the borders of Harvard: there was an identity of interests between all the "oppressed," *i.e.,* professors and students alike, hence they should join against the "exploiters"—the president, deans, and the Corporation. The faculty as a body was unprepared to accept such an analysis. It agreed to set up a committee to propose changes within the decision-making structure of the university and to let student representatives of those organizations which might be interested in the subject under discussion attend faculty deliberations.

At this time, as it happens in revolutionary situations, excitement overflowed its institutional (and even "issue") bounds and became general. It reached into the deepest recesses of laboratories and the studies where scholars and scientists, hitherto oblivious of any issues and who had not attended any faculty or committee meetings for years, now became aware of the gathering storm outside. In a sense the anguished student—the revolutionary—had achieved his primary goal; he had been noticed and communicated his excitement to a wider circle. Had the university been able to preserve that institutional privacy (*not* isolation) which had been its good fortune to have until about 1960 or so, then most likely the wave of excitement would have subsided, and the forces of tradition, routine, and common sense would have reasserted themselves. But now the merciless glare of public attention had been fixed on the campus. The university was supposed to provide news and, in a way, public amusements. For an aspiring Democratic politician, campus unrest was a signal measure of the failure of the first Republican administration, which had just come into office. For a conservative spokesman it was a convenient whip with which to chastise the academic world as responsible for having brought America to its present low estate. What fertile material for sermons and for television! Could one recall a single television program about Einstein, about the vastly (but, alas, peacefully) changing university scene in the fifties? Now campus disorders appeared almost providentially to take up the slack created on news programs by the abatement in urban riots and on the drama side by the public's weariness with Westerns and those gruesome serials about doctors.

Under such pressures it was becoming difficult for the most phlegmatic student to remain uninvolved. Was he being a traitor to his generation? Did he then approve of the U.S. policies in Vietnam? Conversely, many a bookish or withdrawn professor was now bound to feel a strange exhilaration. It was some kind of bliss to be middle-aged and to be asked by the young not just questions about physiology or economics but about life, America and university policies. In fact, some of those who had made the student and his concerns their field of study found themselves superseded in the limelight of the college drama by complete laymen, *i.e.,* physicists or geologists who had not written a single paper on adolescence or peer groups. When the above-mentioned faculty-student committee was formed, a clinical psychologist felt impelled to write a letter to a newspaper pointing out with indignation that it did not contain a single person *professionally* qualified to deal with students' psyches and problems.

Excited people are drawn to a place which promises excitement. Thus, as the spring of 1969 neared, Harvard Square became a point of attraction for youths seeking adventure and vivifying spectacles. It had for some time been a considerable center for dissemination of drugs. Now it also became an assembly point for various cults and radical offshoots of what we have been persuaded was the youth culture. Papers and pamphlets with the most bizarre content but also with the most monotonous vocabulary—and all incorrectly described as an underground press—were hawked in the same location. One group of outsiders consisting, I believe, of veterans of the Columbia battle (of the preceding spring) began to disrupt some college classes, lectures and classroom proceedings. At first they encountered only a confused response on the part of professors and students. Thus victimized, some lecturers tried to engage the intruders in a dialogue with results which can well be imagined. Students even of the most radical persuasion viewed such activities with disapproval. Why, then, one might ask, didn't *they* do something about it? Well, explained one disapproving student, that would have meant interfering with other people's freedom to protest. The turbulent visitors believed, quite logically from their point of view, that all the talk about issues within the university was a lot of nonsense. One had to strike at the root of repressive authority, *i.e.*, the professor's presumption that he had the right to lecture while the students had to listen. While engaged in this task of liberating Harvard students from any residue of the superstitious awe of the teacher-oppressor, the troop was lodged in students' rooms in one of the houses. Their hosts, it turned out later, had disapproved all along of their guests and their activities. But could one refuse shelter to people who needed it just because one disapproved of their *politics?*

What were we all doing, *i.e.*, students and teachers, who felt strongly about such goings-on? Why, we were signing petitions, expressing indignation, and asserting our faith in reasoned discourse as the cornerstone of academic freedom.

Eventually the disrupters were arrested and charged with trespass. During the trial their leader confided amiably to my friend, whose course had been a special target of those activities, that this had come to him as a surprise. Disruptions of a similar character were occurring now regularly at other universities. But college administrators hesitated to invoke the help of the civil authorities. There was a warning in what had happened at Columbia. Some even found comfort in this new expression of dissent: *finally* the extremists were showing their true colors; the great bulk of moderate students was bound to disapprove of such tampering with learning, that is if one exhibited patience and refrained from action which might be deemed "provocative" (such as calling in the police). Besides, as the president of a distinguished and large university explained, only a *small* percentage of classess at his institution were being thus disrupted.

The drift of events was unmistakable. Some sort of major disturbance was clearly in the offing. The actual sequence of events in a situation of this kind is of lesser importance than the fact of growing excitement which, barring some very unusual turn of events, must find a catalyst. The faculty grimly addressed itself to the issue of ROTC. I recall but dimly the discussion which touched on some intricate technical questions—it was not only the matter for faculty of arts and sciences but for other faculties which also had students in reserve officers training organizations; whether the Pentagon would agree to retain ROTC at Harvard if its courses were stripped of academic credit, and so on. But there was at least one speech upbraiding the university for its complicity in the misdeeds of American imperialism and another in which the speaker declared that he had voted for Mr. Lyndon Johnson in 1964, and then the president, evidently unmindful of that fact, led us into a sordid war, all of which he believed added up to an argument against retaining ROTC at Harvard. The faculty voted to divest ROTC courses of academic credit and its officers of their membership. Seemingly the Issue was resolved: the U.S. government was punished, the ROTC disestablished.

Ah, but was it? The faculty could but propose, the corporation had to dispose. Usually the governing body would, as a matter of course, ratify such a decision after taking into account views of other faculties concerned. But could one trust the corporation? There was the business of negotiations with the Defense Department, of phasing out ROTC or conversely of it being retained as an extracurricular activity. There was a possibility of further tricks on the part of the academic establishment to retain militarism on the campus. A sociologist, reputedly wise in the ways of young radicals, had even before the faculty vote suggested submitting the whole problem to a student referendum. This was a *formalistic* view of democracy, and as is well known, such referenda in the past and at other institutions did not result in a victory for the enlightened and progressive position.

Thus the Issue refused to die and kept bobbing up to the surface of our turbulence. The president of the university was testifying before the *SFAC* when a group of radical students entered and some of them yelled insults at him. One could view this incident as a way of testing (probably unconsciously on the part of those participating) the limits of the university's tolerance. To nobody's particular surprise it was discovered, once again, that they stretched.

On April 9 after a student meeting in the Yard, a group entered the University Hall and invited university officials to get out, ejecting some of them by force. After several hours the police were summoned and cleared the building, also by force, the event which passed into Harvard history as the University Hall "bust." In discussing this event at a subsequent faculty meeting, a friend of mine compared it to the smashing of a wonderful work of art. Emotionally (and it was to be a very emotion-ridden period for some time), one sympathized with such anguish. But it is doubtful whether for some time past the American university could have been described as a work of art. And perhaps it is wrong to think of it as such even in its periods of tranquility. It was meant to be the key institution of our culture. And culture has been defined in a recent and very wise book as "an element passed down from generation to generation—a product of continuity without which life would break up in chaos. . . ."*

---

*Nadezhda Mandelstam, *Hope Against Hope: A Memoir*, translated from Russian by Max Hayward (New York: Atheneum, 1970), p. 266.

5

After the Fall

ON THAT APRIL DAY in 1969 when small—at first—groups of students began to enter Harvard's administrative building and to eject various officials and secretaries, many in and around the university felt a deep shock of horror and of fulfillment. The action was but the latest and, in some ways, not the most objectionable in the series of incidents directed against the university, *i.e.*, in violation of its rules and conventions. But people who were not particularly moved by the forcible detention of one person (as in the Dow episode) now felt in the wake of the forcible ejection of deans and the student occupation of University Hall that their world had come to an end. Harvard had turned out to be not all that different from Columbia, from Wisconsin, Cornell and from those other institutions of (as they are known) higher learning. The activities figured in the box score of student disorders now regularly reported in several national newspapers. Taking over a building had become of late a sort of accreditation to the growing association of American universities in trouble. A college where a building had not been seized was that year looked at with a certain awe—what was this special magic which its administrators possessed? Was it an almost superhuman gift of communicating with their students?—but also with a certain degree of suspicion: were they telling the whole truth? Thus, Yale had not had a seizure, but the envious rumored that one of its buildings had been set on fire. Yet the fire might have been accidental, or if arson were to be proved, it could still be the work of a single demented individual.

Though the event had been foreseeable and foreseen, there had been no clear-cut stratagem developed to cope with it. This would have been difficult for, by now, there had developed a body of folk wisdom about what must *not* be done in such grievous circumstances. Thus, the naive might have argued that the best plan was the simplest one, namely an announcement that if a building were to be occupied the university would forthwith call for help to clear it. But such an announcement would have been viewed by some faculty members, among other things, as a clear provocation. Then one assumed the responsible officials should have announced that if the university were prevented from normal functioning—and if they were not supposed to summon the police—well, then, the university would stop functioning until such time as it could start functioning again. Even a worse provocation many would have exclaimed: the *administration* proposes to punish the great mass of moderate students for misdeeds of a few extremists. Besides, one should not underestimate the ingenuity and legalistic skills of the young. It was to be argued subsequently that the occupied building was devoted entirely to administrative labors. How, then, did the act interfere in any way with the essential purposes of the university which are those of teaching and learning? Thus, one might dare say it would not have helped had the faculty passed the motion which was offered at a meeting before the crisis but never acted upon because other business intervened; and, for obvious reasons, it was not taken up at subsequent meetings. Still the motion bespoke the times we live in. It would have put the faculty on record as regarding as "unacceptable any attempt to obstruct normal University procedures, or to cause damage to the property of the University or its members, whatever the motives for such action might be."

With University Hall now occupied, we were all thrown into anxious deliberations about what must not be done. In the folklore of confrontation there was the tale of one university administration which outwaited the occupiers until, tired and demoralized, they withdrew. But at Harvard, because of its location, the building could not be sealed off or isolated. Also, a rumor arose (which was to turn out to be true) that various confidential papers were being purloined from the deans' safes and photographed. There was to be, subsequently, some criticism that those papers had not been removed to a safer place; but the logic inherent in that complaint would have led eventually to the university transferring its administrative operations to an underground bunker.

Then, theoretically, the university administration could capitulate to the demands in the name of which the occupation of the building was perpetrated. There were such demands though subsequently they were forgotten except for one about the Issue *i.e.*, an immediate removal of ROTC, and a demand that Harvard forsake the expansion of its Medical School's facilities since that would have involved the destruction of some housing in a poor quarter of Boston. But connoisseurs of confrontation, including even fairly radical ones, were unanimous in holding that a capitulation *before* the seized building was evacuated was one of those things which must *not* be done.

The building had been occupied, we were told, by people

wise in such matters, by the Chinese-oriented faction of
Students for a Democratic Society. (What, by the way, would a
visitor from another planet or even country have made of this
statement which was assumed to be self-explanatory?) But
afterwards it was entered and inhabited by various students—
and non-students—who were far from being supporters of
Comrade Mao. With portraits of former presidents and deans
staring down upon them in the large faculty room, the
assembled occupiers passed the resolution that no pot should
be smoked (reportedly leading to bitter comments as to how
a movement which is allegedly for liberation makes "repression" its first order of business). Notwithstanding such
limitations on personal freedom, some participants in the
take-over claimed subsequently that they experienced a
strong emotion of a shared venture and danger, and that
quite apart from any politics involved. One who, by the way,
left before the police arrived on the scene, was to write
ecstatically that he felt a "bond of community," of being
"among brothers and sisters," an emotion which made all the
more vivid how exploited and deprived he had been during
his previous existence as an upper-middle-class adolescent.
There were, finally, individuals who wandered in through
sheer curiosity.

The decision of the president and deans to summon the
police was probably affected by this multifarious use to
which University Hall was being put and which made it quite
likely that it could be occupied almost indefinitely by rotating
garrisons; and by its central location, due to which it
could and did attract interested citizens from Greater Boston,
not to mention the youth of neighboring high schools who
passed through Harvard Yard and were being treated to a
tantalizing glimpse of higher education. The "must not"
about the police was thus countered by the "must not"
about a lingering occupation. And, finally, the police arrived

in the early morning hours of the next day, cleared the building, beat some students, arrested more, quite a few.

This again completely transformed the situation. What had been a mini-revolution now ended, or at least subsided, and was replaced by a wave of quasi-religious hysteria, which in a mini-fashion—thank God—was analogous to such great emotional tremors of the past as, one supposes, the St. Vitus dance in the Middle Ages, or some particularly hysteria-laden episodes during various modern political and religious revolutions. Such periods bring into sharp relief the obvious inability of any rationally conceived civilization to allow for the deeply-held human need to release strong emotions and anxieties in what might be called a tribal manner. For the few days following the police "bust" (as it is known in the liturgy of student dissent), there was a quasi-rational veneer over what every component group within the university was doing. The president, fellows, and the other, larger governing body, the overseers, met, discussed the situation, issued statements. Radical students came forth with various sets of non-negotiable demands; moderate students proclaimed a strike until *their* demands, apparently negotiable, were conceded. The faculty was meeting almost uninterruptedly, for in addition to its sessions as a body twice a week, a considerable number spent intervening periods in various committees, caucuses, writing and revising resolutions, etc. But all such activities, one suspected, were almost beside the point insofar as the main need of those more deeply agitated was concerned: which was for some form of *physical* expression of their feelings in which they would be joined by others. One felt like making the grotesque and indecorous suggestion that the hysteria could be alleviated if, in a large open space at an appointed hour, the president and fellows of Harvard College burst into a ritualist dance, then to be joined by professors and concerned students, the dance to continue until the participants collapsed in utter exhaustion.

The young men who were angry were mostly—or so I suspected—angry not so much for any political reason, or even because of the "bust," but because they felt (unjustifiably, in many cases) that their elders were not as agitated as they. Since our culture does not provide for a ritualistic dance in which old as well as young can join (as a matter of fact some performing ensembles did come to Harvard Yard during that week and one, if I recall correctly, snake-danced through a university building) all we could do was to *talk*. At the end of one faculty meeting which lasted more than four hours and left several older and middle-aged professors close to physical and emotional prostration, a representative of concerned undergraduates stood up and announced that this was a good *beginning*. We were all requested to join various groups of concerned students and to continue the dialogue.

My blurred impressions of the next few days refer mostly to "talk." Hell, one concluded, must be a place where there is a continuous teach-in or debate going on, while the agenda of purgatory is mostly committee meetings always drafting, revising and withdrawing resolutions. One began to understand how much progress in rationalism and liberalism has consisted in people mastering the urge to talk, and acquiring self-discipline to speak to the point and sparsely, and requiring the same discipline from those to whom they would listen. It is, perhaps, the basic characteristic of a totalitarian society that those who rule it, no matter how enlightened, will never surrender—and constantly exercise—their power to hector, warn, and admonish, in brief to pester and bore their helpless subjects. In our own situation, however, talk became the almost inevitable mechanism for exorcising the accumulated excitement; and so we were admonished, warned and exhorted from various sources; and, depending on our aptitude for those pursuits, engaged in them ourselves.

Much of the oratory was repetitious. People rose to speak in anguish and sat down hopefully. One word which was being constantly repeated was "community." With the exception of extremists, everybody agreed that we were or ought to be a community. It would not have done to ask what this convenient and all-purpose word was supposed to mean in the case of a university. Was Harvard a community in the sense of a Trappist monastery, or as in "intellectual community"? The moral earnestness of many would have been offended if they had been told that they were striving for the same meaning which a few years before would have been expressed by a more American and less Hegelian-sounding cliché: "we're all on the same team." But such homely Americanisms now would have been thought inappropriate: a team is a hierarchical organization (coach, captain), at times shading into an authoritarian one ("turn in your uniform"), with discipline and imbued with the competitive—and nowadays, very often mercenary—spirit. When soon there began to be issued a very considerable body of university legislation stipulating all sorts of rules (which previously no one thought needed to be spelled out in writing because, one supposes, there was a tacit community agreement on them), the term "community" proved to be handy and was repeatedly used.

"Legitimacy" ran second to "community" as the word most frequently used. Was the structure of authority within the university legitimate? Now, this calls again for the pedantic but necessary objection to the misuse of language. What people who questioned the "legitimacy" of the Corporation meant was, of course, that they did not like what it was doing or had no confidence in the wisdom or good faith of its decisions. A body of students proclaimed "a strike" until some demands were met. This was an inappropriate term for what was, in fact, a boycott of classes by about, I would judge, fifty to sixty per cent of the undergraduate body, but "strike" sounds better: it evokes the image of the downtrodden and protesting proletarian. The whole bizarre terminology which sprang up pointed up how difficult and artificial it was to apply analogies from politics, or from the field of labor relations, to the university even when stricken by a partly political crisis.

In fact, the word theatre comes to mind when one reflects on various elements in the disturbances. The emotions aroused were intense but they were aroused by something in the nature of theatrical performances. Many photographs of the period look posed though undoubtedly they were not. I recall one of a student meeting in front of the library. Behind the speaker there were several undergraduates holding signs demanding dialogue, communication, an open university. To an amazing degree they were matched insofar as their height, facial adornment and expressions were concerned. I am sure that I did not imagine that many of those who wore a red kerchief tied around the elbow, the emblem of the strike, strolled in a distinctive swaying fashion. There were also some conscious artistic touches to the drama. Students in the School of Design came up with the heraldic device of the revolt which became nationally famous (and it is unimportant whether it was original or not): a red hand, as if dissolving in blood, depicted against a white background on the back of a shirt. This suggested protest against an outrage already perpetrated rather as in the usual Marxist imagery: a fist smiting the oppressor, revolution triumphant. There were mass meetings in the football stadium and even these pictures give the effect of being posed: here the crowd lounges in a Mediterranean manner (the weather collaborated with the drama): there it is angrily defiant in the way one would think of revolutionary Russian sailors and soldiers in

1917; all mixed incongruously with an element of Anglo-Saxon parliamentarianism (chairmen and tellers counting votes). For a few days this usually sedate institution of learning looked like a movie-lot where a story of revolutionary heroics was being filmed. And so if one stayed around those performers too long one ran the risk of being caught in the emotion; you could almost understand and sympathize with the plight of American youth from the upper middle class, with their despair at seeing ahead of them nothing but the vista of an orderly and prosperous career.

ONE WAS RESCUED from such potentially dangerous thoughts by the return, even if only partial, of reality. It surged back in the form of issues, committees, and elections to committees. The student "strike" was called off. It dawned on many, even radical students, that as a stage for revolutionary, perhaps even only political, action the university had several built-in inconveniences. It operates according to seasons, hence political action during an examination period is likely to be most unpopular and in August, say, impossible. There was some thought of overcoming this uncomfortable fact by keeping the nucleus of concerned activists in residence throughout the summer, but then it proved impracticable. Besides the calendar there was one even more basic difficulty which dawned on many: the university may be harassed, shut down, even destroyed, but how can it be *conquered?* Do you install a group of radical students to manage the institution's finances? How can participatory democracy apply in the case of choosing people to teach physics? The out-and-out radical, then, had to shift his fire and begin to denounce the university as a corporate entity and for what it was allegedly doing as a landlord and employer rather than to its students. Many of the breed would thus eventually shift the focus of their activity away from the campus and the classroom, though the

university would remain a convenient symbol of unrighteousness. For others such displacement of the focus of their
emotion would prove impossible. In addition to the war and
the racial problem, other issues or causes were appearing on
the American scene and ripening in the public attention:
women's rights, migratory farm workers, pollution, the
American Indian. The university would be assailed for its
oppression or (equally bad) neglect on those scores.

Faculty actions during the first and the most tense stage of
the crisis mirrored the belief, now a standard part of the
folklore of the student revolution, that the real struggle was
for the confidence of the moderate students. The radical
student, it was held, was a fanatic; he represented but a small
minority of the undergraduate population. He gained in
strength and danger by latching on to issues, provoking the
university to exert force brutally and unwisely and thus
temporarily gaining hold on the great bulk, the moderate
students. Hence it was held wise to detach the "moderates"
from the "extremists." A faculty resolution condemned the
occupation of University Hall, but it also at least implied a
criticism of the administration for calling in the police. The
same body also thought it wise to demand a definite and
unconditional phasing out of ROTC. Finally, a jointly-elected
faculty-student committee was set up to investigate and to
adjudge punishments. All those gestures and enactments were
believed necessary to gain or regain the trust of the moderate
student, and to restore (here comes the magic word)
legitimacy to authority within the university.

It is a moot point whether it was those steps which
enabled the university to quiet down, or whether the
protesting students subsided because of fatigue, the approach
of examinations, and the fear that, as the rumor had it,
the university might indeed be shut down. Crowds in the
yard grew smaller, television crews departed, and newspapers

and magazines shifted their attention to more promisingly troubled campuses. The great Harvard crisis was history.

There have been many attempts to assess causes and lessons of the disturbances. Even as the crisis was in its initial hysterico-theatrical phase, there were already several committees, of the faculty and of the overseers, probing causes, trying to assess the responsibility for the mess and to proclaim its lessons. We might eschew for the moment the eloquent (if clothed in generalities) reports produced by those bodies in favor of what could be described as the voice of the people. At one tense period my taxi driver said, "Don't let *them* do to Harvard what *they* did to Columbia," thus suggesting how deeply cherished, despite all the appearances to the contrary, Harvard was among the good people of Greater Boston and how deep a hold the conspiracy theory of history had among them. Another comment requires a brief introduction. The Harvard Houses, when instituted *c.* 1930, were modeled upon the Oxford-Cambridge colleges. They never developed certain features of those ancient—some might say anti-quated—institutions. But one, an essential one, did take root in New England soil: almost every house acquired at least one faithful retainer who over and above his functions as janitor or night watchman displayed interest and affection for the given house, its students and the faculty associated with it, and who would, I am sure, have scorned the notion that he was a member of a wider community or an exploited proletarian. The crisis hastened the extinction of the breed—how briefly do venerable traditions endure on American soil! But before his disappearance one faithful retainer confided to me his analysis of the sources of the trouble: "*It* all began when the students were allowed not to wear neckties in the dinning hall. . . ."

Both comments deserve attention, and they should not be scorned by those who always seek deeper causes for everything, even when simple ones stare them in the face. *"They"* were the tumultuous forces from the outside; newspapers and politicians, this whole growing breed of bureaucrats and publicists whose main occupation consisted in telling people that they should not be doing things they were doing and liked doing but, rather, something else. The university unwisely opened its doors to *them* and they then crowded in. But whether inside or on the periphery of the educational institutions, they have worked ceaselessly, though in most cases probably unconsciously, to make those institutions reflect their own restlessness.

The argument about manners also deserves to be met otherwise than just with a smile. We have been brainwashed to the point where any insistence on any code of manners and deportment is held to be reactionary and undemocratic. People do not find it absurd when it is the courts which are called upon to adjudicate whether and how far a grade-school principal is entitled to instruct pupils as to their dress.

But in the absence of an agreement on manners and social conventions how difficult it is, apart from everything else, to achieve that goal so devoutly desired by all the up-to-date educational theorists, namely communication. The example of Harvard in the wake of the great distrubance is most illuminating on that count.

AMONG THE COMMITTEES launched in the wake of, and as the consequence of, those grievous events was one on Rights and Responsibilities of Members of the University. It sought to define what those rights and responsibilities were, for it was no longer sufficient to assume that they were self-evident, *e.g.,* that the students had the right to be taught and professors the responsibility to teach. The committee found it simple to define things students must not do, such as to engage in "intense personal harassment of such a character as to amount to grave disrespect for the dignity of others."

Then, in this day of democracy and equality, the committee felt it only fair to define things that the officers of the university must not do. That proved more difficult. One version would have put a solemn obligation on administrators and professors to heed *all* reasonable demands—"confronted with such a demand, an officer must do something; he has no right to do nothing." But this version met obvious objections. One of the most insistent demands addressed to various deans and officials during the recent troubles when they tried to expostulate with the angry young men was that they should perform an act which, were it physically possible, would be most indecorous. Well, that was not a reasonable demand. But what was? Confronted with this conundrum which would have taxed the ingenuity of the most subtle logician, the committee decided merely to place us under an obligation

to be alert to the needs of the University Community,
to give full and fair hearings to reasoned expressions of
grievances; and to respond promptly and in good faith
to such expressions and to widely-expressed needs for
change.

Alas, it was still not very helpful. Was it not better when, without any written and tortuous stipulations, people were just supposed to be courteous and considerate (and insofar as the university was concerned, they usually were so)?

But one should not disparage the work of those people, administrators, students and professors, who sat down to frame a new code of behavior, and who apart from such incursions into trying to define the indefinable, hammered together a structure to replace the old mold which had been broken. Their work certainly helped to confound the worst fears of the pessimists who, like myself, at one point did not see how the university could go on. Committees assuage passions.

One must still express some apprehension about the

American university now no longer in the grip of revolution but in that of committees. The source of that apprehension may be best elucidated by quoting two excerpts from the aforesaid resolution on Rights and Responsibilities passed by the Faculty of Arts and Sciences at Harvard. It starts: "The central functions of the academic community are learning, teaching, research and scholarship." Then it goes on to state:

the University must affirm, assure and protect the rights of its members to organize and join political associations, convene and conduct public meetings, and picket in orderly fashion, advocate and publicize opinion by print, sign and voice.

One may be pardoned for asking: why? Those are rights which in our society are guaranteed by the state, and if they were not there would be very little any university could do to keep them operative. In fact, the university does not have the resources to protect *political* rights of its members. Today, on its own, it could not protect the right of certain right-wing politicians, or for that matter of certain members of the present Administration to speak undisturbed on the campus; tomorrow it may not be able to do so in regard to a left-wing extremist.

But the statement is of dubious validity even as a declaration of intent. It is entirely conceivable, as a matter of fact, that this is what has been happening: that the most uncontroversial and laudable *political* activities could reach such an intensity that they would interfere with and frustrate those "central functions" of the university so eloquently defined in the beginning. It is difficult to see why college authorities should not have discretionary power to ban a meeting on its premises even if it is to be held on behalf of the most worthwhile cause and in the most orderly fashion, if in their judgment it would interfere with the regular functioning of the school. If what is going on within the university is as important to society as it is often alleged, as important, say, as what is going on in a hospital, why should anything be allowed to interfere with it?

All members of the University have the right to press for action on matters of concern by any appropriate means.

One feels impelled to cry no! Everybody has concerns which whether individual, social or cosmic transcend the importance of any university regulations. But where would we all be if each of us started simultaneously to press for them, even if by the most appropriate means?

In brief, the university, while in no immediate danger of being destroyed through violence (and it is prudent to keep one's fingers crossed on that), may yet be slowly choked by worthy causes. Issues could go on propagating; the university's resources and the attention of its staff would be increasingly absorbed by various real or spurious social concerns; and students, their attention being continuously drawn to various social ills which it is their urgent responsibility to solve (and *now*) would grow increasingly confused through conflicting claims on their time and excitability. Those students and professors who enjoy their work for its own sake would then tend to withdraw from the main currents of university life; they would become—as the phrase went about those Russian intellectuals who under Tsarism (and now under the Soviets) withdrew from the brutality and fraudulence of society around them—"internal émigrés." Hopefully, there are several signs entitling us to believe that all that shall not come to pass, but the danger certainly is there.

WE ARE, THUS, BACK to the crux of the problem, namely: society does not believe that what has been defined here as the central function of the university—to use one word, learning—is important for its own sake. And how can it, if the academic community itself has doubts on that score?

Such doubts are inherent in the very insistence that the

university is a community. For implied in that definition is the plea that it should be preserved and protected not because there is a lot of useful and necessary work going on there but because association with it bestows some special moral quality. This claim of moral purity, a suggestion that it is somehow an enclave of virtue in the sinful adult world, is well conveyed in our declaration:

> . . .a community ideally characterized by free expression, free inquiry, intellectual honesty, respect for the dignity of others, and openness to constructive change.

Well, you might have an academic community whose members from the president to janitors were amply endowed with those characteristics, and yet which would be worthless, because its faculty was incompetent or distracted from their proper pursuits.

Those moralistic rumblings reflect, then, the deep-seated doubt whether the intellectual endeavor is justifiable for its own sake, and whether those who engage in it deserve protection and respect unless they show themselves morally superior to the common run of adult mankind.

There is yet another and more excusable reason for the moralistic bathos which has currently enveloped our educational institutions. Sentimentality in connection with universities has for a long time been unfashionable. It was held appropriate to an era when the Yale football coach could tell his players on the eve of the Harvard game that nothing in their subsequent life could surpass in importance what they were going to do the next day; in other words, of the time when prestigious universities were, so to speak, educationally oriented country clubs. For a long time, and especially after World War II, such sentimental pomposity was paraded only at alumni meetings, and mostly those attended by the older generations. Otherwise, one talked of one's college with a certain air of realism, if not understatement. One did not rhapsodize about the new breed of Yale or Brown men; one mentioned interesting discoveries being made by some faculty members or that valuable collection acquired by the library. There was an implicit understanding that those were the things which contributed to the students developing into interesting personalities and embarking upon useful careers, and not some waves of sympathy and moralizing emanating from a *guru*-like teacher or a "character-building" coach. But the crisis—the threat to the institution with which one has been associated—loosened those inhibitions against sentimentality and pomposity. One groped for some mystic bond or communion which would bring us all together and save our university. Many a faculty speaker during the Harvard crisis felt constrained to preface his remarks by an avowal of his own personal problem, and of the moral illumination these tragic events were imparting to him. In the post-crisis and less emotionally charged atmosphere, the university still remained a moral entity, rather than a utilitarian institution. One takes pride in what *this* university is doing for social justice and how *its* faculty stands as one with the students in daring the Establishment to do its worst.

And so the old character-building college has returned. Make no mistake: that nationally-known sociologist who explains so convincingly the "sources of alienation" is a reincarnation of the dean or coach who knew how to communicate with the young, who showed them not only how to be students and players, but above all, men. And the new student hero extolled by an alumni magazine—he whose three-hundred-page report on reforming the college curriculum has drawn students away from the extremists and into the avenues of constructive change—look at him for awhile, and his disheveled form dissolves and then reassembles as Dick Stover of Yale, infusing a demoralized team with his infectious enthusiasm and himself scoring the decisive touchdown.

THE AMERICAN UNIVERSITY OF TODAY is infinitely more important to its students, to the nation and the world then was the case in 1900 or 1925. And so the current wave of intellect-numbing sentimentalizing and moralizing about its role and responsibilities is not only amusing but disturbing. What George Orwell wrote in 1939 is, alas, only too true of the American scene today:

We have now sunk to a depth at which the restatement
of the obvious is the first duty of intelligent men.*

But so many intelligent men today are afraid to restate the obvious without mixing it with some fashionable nonsense; and especially when it comes to education, they do it undoubtedly in the conviction that otherwise they would not be listened to at all, that the great thing is to "communicate" and thus to avoid trouble for the moment, and in the end, common sense is bound to return. But on the last score Orwell also has a timely warning: ". . . And yet the peculiar horror of the present moment is that we cannot be sure that this is so." We cannot be sure that the university will limp through the era of "constructive change" and yet emerge in the end still recognizable as a university.

The debate concerning the nature and purpose of higher education is allegedly between liberals and conservatives: those who believe in change, and those who want to stand pat, between people who see in education an instrument of social justice and for achievement of real democracy, and the believers in an elitist university narrowly academic, deaf to wider social issues and grievances. But in point of fact nothing could be more false. Traditionally it has been the conservative who has been dissatisfied with the notion of the university just propagating knowledge, the reactionary who has seen that function as unimportant in comparison with its

---

*George Orwell, "An Age Like This," *The Collected Essays, Journalism and Letters of George Orwell*, Vol. 1, ed. by Sonia and Angus Orwell (New York: Harcourt Brace Jovanovich, 1968), p. 375.

obligations to society, namely the moral and religious upbringing of its students. Conversely, it is the liberal who has demanded that the university be free not only of the government but of the religious and political passions of the day, not because it is or ought to be more virtuous than the surrounding community or immune to its laws, but because otherwise it could not do its proper job. It has been the conservative who has tended to be the busybody where education is concerned, the liberal the defender of what is derisively known as the ivory tower concept. In fact, the liberal has never worried (and with good reason) that under modern conditions the university, if it stuck to its job, would or could become isolated from society or become anything but a force for progress. If it helps its students to learn mathematics, languages and economics, if it expands knowledge, then it has to be a force for moral and material advance, be its faculty most detached from the proverbial issues of the day, its trustees most reactionary, its student body thoroughly apathetic concerning politics. The modern university, unlike its medieval counterpart, has become a force for progress and liberty precisely because it has been able to detach itself from the moralistic passions and fashions of the day, and thus liberate intellects and energies of its members for the acquisition and expansion of knowledge, rather than allowing them to be imprisoned in moralistic introspection and spiritual conundrums. The road to the Dark Ages runs precisely through "constructive change" as it is often argued: the university as an institution which is completely attuned to the political, social and religious agitation of the surrounding world; its professors and students abandoning laboratories and libraries and running out into the streets at every even minor domestic or foreign crisis, and spending the intervals in unavoidably inconclusive debates as to the rights and wrongs of every issue and cause which has gained a handful of adherents in their midst.

One therefore grows uneasy at much of the current debate about restructuring the university. Among the committees which have been produced by the Harvard crises, there has been one on the Governance of the University. In due course it has come up with what is described as a discussion memorandum on The Nature and Purposes of the University.* And here one reads:

> With a renewed sense of the values and purposes of the university we can approach the difficult task of changing our governance structure to cope with the multiple challenges ... If such approaches are to achieve their purpose of helping Harvard provide leadership in this crisis period, they must be accompanied by a searching debate that engages the entire community in a confrontation of new issues and basic questions.

Vagueness and orotundity are at times valuable polemical and political devices. One recalls their masterful use by Queen Elizabeth I when fighting for time and pressed by Parliament to effect basic changes in the governance of England, *i.e.,* to get married. And in more recent times the same technique served well President Eisenhower and Casey Stengel when confronted with troublesome questions at their respective press conferences. But one cannot accuse the distinguished faculty members and concerned students who drafted the memorandum of *studied* vagueness. This *is* the idiom of committees which all over the country are working at restructuring and redefining purposes, of editorials in serious papers on those and related questions, on what the presidential and other commissions have to say on the subject. All of which is rather scary.

---

*Who says that the printing machine cannot make a Freudian slip? Through the omission of one word, "Committee," the memorandum almost appeared to have taken power: it is identified on its title page as having come from the University of Governance, Harvard University.

"Restructuring" is to lead us to the university of the future which will be based on legitimacy, relevance and participation, and which will banish elitism, competitiveness and thus, hopefully, alienation. The opaqueness of those aims reflects, it is fair to say, what people who talk in such terms assume the students want. But since all those terms are incapable of precise definition, the effort to achieve those lofty aims must of necessity lead to continuous "searching discussion" *i.e.,* a proliferation of committees, debates, and so on. How does that help? Shall we reach the point, and how would we know when we had, when alienation will have been abolished and the generation gap bridged? Will nonsense become unfashionable only when its consequences are so disastrous that people will sigh for the good old days when we were worrying only about alienation and the generation gap. It is already conceivable that private universities may collapse financially before too long; and it is at least problematic whether and for how long society, *i.e.,* various legislatures, would be inclined to assume the burden. Let us not forget that today's alienated are tomorrow's taxpayers, and they may not wish to spend money to put another generation through what they have suffered.

But Cassandras are not effective in changing the social climate of their times. They may help impart general gloom, but they do not instill caution when they descend to specifics (such as asking where will the money come from). And so perhaps the road to improvement and some stability must lead through restructurings and redefinitions.

If so, one must ask for concreteness in all those endeavors, and for an estimation of costs (economic, social and intellectual) of the proposed and contemplated reforms. Otherwise, we shall never cut short the circular flow of vapid generalities, and the continuous proliferation of committees, as well as the university's assuming new tasks and responsibilities which, if they do not speed its financial bankruptcy, will still hasten its transformation into a community center rather than a school.

Take "alienation." Can it be combatted by making academic studies "relevant," *i.e.,* by making what he does in college "meaningful" to the student? Would we not also have to drop the whole elitist concept of college education? Here is a fair sample of the quicksand one steps in when one engages in today's educational discourse. I have known persons who have been entirely swallowed up by it, persons previously of the most precise turn of mind and habits of speech who after a few weeks' immersion in committees and resolutions, themselves sound even in ordinary conversation, like memoranda and resolutions. The current and frequent usage of what used to be obscene words must be due in some part to the need to escape that terrible burden of vagueness and sententiousness which has descended upon us.

But we must persevere. "Alienation" is a term much bandied around and most people assume that it is synonymous with aggravated boredom, a state vaguely similar to that which one experiences when listening to dull conversation while suffering from indigestion. But there is, of course, real alienation close to what Hegel and Marx tried to convey by the term: the feeling that one's work does not express one's personality, the despair about leaving one's individual imprint upon the world. Therefore, if it lies at all within the resources of a school to combat alienation, it must be through the development of individual capacities and interests. The study of even the most esoteric subject may dissipate alienation insofar as it leads the student to become engrossed in it, and to try to leave his imprint upon it. In contrast, a subject of the highest social importance may yet be bereft of any intellectual content and offer no scope for the individual's intellectual contribution. Nuclear disarmament is very important for our future; eighteenth-century Spanish literature is not. But what can a course on nuclear disarmament offer except to repeat in various ways that we had better find a technique of limiting and eventually eliminating nuclear weapons or otherwise we would come to a very bad end? Relevance is, then, as it is currently understood, a false god. It confuses things we should worry about with things we should study. And, fair enough, had mankind always pursued that precept—had we always studied mainly the things we ought to be deeply concerned about— we would have no alienation for we would have no civilization whatever.

Our committees on restructuring should, then, pursue this specific problem: Has our education become relevant to the point where it is ceasing to be meaningful to a large segment of students? Are young men and women required as part of their expensive higher education to sit through lectures on what they already know and hear incessantly from newspapers, television, from each other? Perhaps part of their dissatisfaction proceeds from the inadequate scope being provided for their intellectual curiosity, from being lured into fields and courses where one chews over and over the same issues, causes, and anxieties. Perhaps watery generalization is at least as debilitating and irritating as educational fare as that pedantic specialization, "learning more and more about less and less," which used to be an accusation brought against higher education.

One cannot dispose of this suspicion by simply pointing out that among the dissatisfied students and professors are those in mathematics as well as in sociology and divinity, people with strong intellectual interests as well as those with just anxieties. But apart from statistics there is the matter of the general climate of opinion, or in plain English of a lot of people telling the young what they "really" *ought* to want. Witness the general surprise and shock when one of those absurd polls comes up with the shattering conclusion that young Americans are not all that different from what young people always have been.

If only those new generalities contained *half* truths! But sometimes they are wholly misleading or completely meaningless. What is one to make of a statement I read in one of our current committee reports that young Americans "by their actions as well as their words . . . are moving their value emphasis from private well being to public well being"? There is a whole number of nonsensical or mischievous meanings which could be read into this single statement: public well being can in no sense be identified as a sum of individuals' well being; if you don't care how well off you are, you contribute to the general welfare; most young Americans believe that by being on the public payroll or that of various foundations they can best contribute to the growth of national wealth and its more just division.

But generalities and rhetoric are usually harmless, you might say; and can a cogent and beneficial document which strives to enunciate some principles escape them entirely? But we have witnessed in our recent educational history how quickly rhetoric and generalities become transmuted into academic programs endowed with budgets and students and professors. Here is the official Harvard University *Gazette* recently announcing what has come to be called an innovationist program:

> According to the program's prospectus, graduates will assume *upper level* positions in government, foundations, and private profit and non-profit research organizations . . . some will become involved in politics while many others will devote their energies toward changing existing bureaucratic structures . . . the more adventuresome in spirit will seek to establish new *experimental* modes of living as a way of attracting others to *healthier* interpersonal reactions. (Italics added.)

The program's director is quoted as saying about the prospective students: "All of them are frustrated by trying to change the world and have come back for more powerful tools."

One must, then, agree that much of alienation and of the *unwarranted* elitist feeling about the university is produced on the premises. But the road away from them leads not through ever-greater vagueness or the university forging ever more powerful tools to change a society which evidently refuses to heed the precepts of Professor *X* or Dean *Y*. Both the scholar and the activist would feel their alienation seep away as they acquire actual intellectual skills such as languages or science, and develop curiosity about an intricate historical or literary problem rather than pondering over and over again how sick our society is or "raising fundamental questions concerning the meaning of life" (which, as the Minute on the Nature and Purposes of the University instructs us, is what young Americans, presumably unlike young people in other cultures and generations, are currently doing).

There is a right kind of elitism and competitiveness and a wrong one when it comes to university education. We have just seen an example of the wrong kind, of a silly (and, in a democracy, also a dangerous) presumption that here in the university you can train people not in specific skills but in some special wisdom on how society ought to be run. But the acquisition of a skill, be it that of an engineer, basketball player or social worker, is of necessity an elitist endeavor, and the process of acquiring it, equally necessarily, is a competitive one.

Few points about the educational process would seem to be more self-evident, to call less for elaboration. But in the present climate of opinion this is precisely one of the main battlegrounds on which the struggle for a restructuring and redefinition of the university is raging. Grades and examinations—those are, if you please, undemocratic devices, the means by which society conditions the young to accept their role as cogs in the vast machine of competition and exploitation through which it strips them of their natural instinct for altruism and cooperation. In some colleges, grades have been virtually abolished. There is considerable pressure in the same direction in the graduate schools. Isn't it more important for a lawyer or doctor to be filled with zeal for social change, with solicitude for the poor, than to be a master of his craft?

The present lamentable trend is different from the traditional strain of distrust of higher education as such, the somewhat natural reaction of a populistic democracy that it is better to be a good man than a highly educated one, that university education gives people airs, etc. The full horror of the current educational ideology lies in the fact that carried to its logical conclusion it would have everybody go through four years of college and yet make that college largely useless insofar as the acquisition of knowledge and skills is concerned. It is fashionable nowadays and considered profound to ask "Education for What?" And indeed there should be places where people so inclined should pursue this interesting subject as well as those other "fundamental questions concerning the meaning of life." And once they have found answers they should be allowed to emerge from their seclusion and resume their place in the university as administrators and professors. But not before.

The harassed educators would probably complain that this is unfair. They are fighting a rear-guard action against the students' demands and those are the things the youth want. But are they? In reading some of the more coherent student-authored disquisitions on education and life, it becomes at once apparent how deeply derivative and tired their notions are, whether it comes to criticisms of the traditional university, or portraying the one in the brave new world of concern and activism. Usually those are echoes and scraps of Marx, Freud, or Jung (all of whom would be on the "square" side in today's educational debate), as chewed over, vulgarized, or distorted by some currently fashionable popularizers of those worthies. Or even worse, what passes for the authentic voice of the youth reflects the hair-raising banalities of the symposia, panels, and commissions of the "where do we go from here" and "what do the young want" variety. Thus it is unfair to classify such efforts as juvenile outpourings; their authors, mostly unconsciously, repeat what the befuddled segment of middle-aged in middle-class America expects to hear from the young. The famous dialogue is, for the most part, a recitation in unison.

It is difficult to be very hopeful about the present efforts to restructure and redefine the university as long as those engaged in them view their task as mainly that of public relations rather than policy, as long as their objective is to secure or restore calm to the campuses rather than reason to educational theory and practice. Parallels with politics are in this connection misleading. In public life rhetoric and generalities may, though not without exacting an eventual price, still be useful in assuaging passions of the moment. Concessions to currently popular fads and superstititions are not irrevocable, for people will sooner or later feel their effect and in a democratic society will be able to undo or curb harmful policies. But the consequences of concessions to nonsense and obscurantism in educational matters are always bound to be long-lasting, and in some cases a permanent blight on personalities which have been exposed to them while young. A school which yields to fads and allows its pupils to have as their field of study worrying about social and ethical problems and thus deprives them of the opportunity to master or develop an abiding interest in sciences, languages, or literatures, also deprives them of that intellectual capital they will need and miss whatever their future careers as businessmen, radicals, or reformers.

WHAT CAN BE SAID about student manners and morals and discipline—this is the area of academic life where we are witnessing the most insistent claims for student freedom and power (the two are incorrectly and incautiously assumed to be synonymous) and the most rapid growth of personnel, for as rules and regulations disappear there is evidently need for ever greater numbers of people to administer them.

Here there is obviously a world of difference about the situation in colleges as against lower schools. There, to abolish the authority of the school over the student's deportment is a blow to education itself. But no such tragic results need follow from the university devolving the responsibility for such matters to the students themselves. But here is the catch: such devolution, if desirable at all, should be complete. It obviously makes little sense for deans or faculty residents to inhabit and exercise nominal supervision over student dormitories, if in fact they have no authority and if their functions are essentially assimilated to those of hotel-keepers or their social directors. There has been a trend, for instance, publicly hailed by all and viewed with secret horror by some, toward co-educational dormitories in many of our bastions of higher learning. But whatever one's aesthetic reservations about premature domesticity, there is no reason why such weighty matters as numerical proportions of sexes in the given building, their domestic arrangements and facilities, could not be handled entirely by students rather than taking up the time and attention of people who could be more fruitfully occupied in studying and teaching early English poetry or nuclear physics.

In fact, the same principle might be extended to other areas where vociferous claims are made for student participation and where there are no technical reasons why truly representative student committees and bureaucracy could not perform the tasks now handled so diffidently by paid administrators. What one has, increasingly, is an impasse in the form of mixed committees, *i.e.*, the situation where trustees or administrators still bear all the responsibility and the burden of administrative and fiscal management of university affairs, but often without having the sufficient power, or (what amounts to the same thing) self-confidence, to follow their better judgment. Perhaps in this day of educational experimentation there is room for a new type of university where the whole non-academic side of its management, including securing money from public or private sources, would be in the hands of representative student organs.

Such ideas are not likely to curry favor with advocates even of the most radical restructuring of the university. Many of them indeed would view such suggestions as an attempt to ridicule the whole notion of student participation. But how, barring experiments in that direction, could one assess the willingness of students to shoulder some of the administrative burdens and decision-making, and thus incidentally also to lighten the financial cost of their education? And in the absence of such readiness it is impossible to believe that "student power" is what the students want.

Much of even the structural side of the debate on higher education makes one wonder whether all those people who talk and write with such passion about it really wish to resolve the problem. Isn't their idea of an interesting university one in which there is constant tension, constant uncertainty as to who is to do what and why? If by some miracle national politics were to calm down, if we are not called upon to demonstrate about this or that burning issue, then there is still the enticing prospect of constant wrangling about how the university is to invest its money, what proportion of students and faculty is to serve on this or that committee, what is relevant, etc. We would all still be denied the freedom, a very basic one, of going about our own business.

But we must not imagine that we can advance very far in coping with the present crisis just by trying to identify the villain as a group, profession, or generation. Even those who derive their livelihood or sense of mission from distracting the university from its proper functions and from stirring the anxieties of the young are also victims of their own rhetoric and anxieties and would be in most cases happier, and perhaps even materially as well off, in more constructive pursuits. It is the moralistic rhetoric which is the villain. It triggers off that incongruous mixture of idealism, restlessness, and brutality which is just as evident in the impulses which have led to our universities becoming crippled as to those which have led to the tragedy of Vietnam.

OF ALL THE FORMS of addiction, the one to platitudes may yet prove the most insidious and dangerous. It strikes at all age levels. Traditionally, politicians, educators and newspaper editorial writers have been the most susceptible, but in recent years it has exacted an increasing toll among the young. As with other forms of addiction, it distorts the sense of reality: hazy images take the place of concrete objects. Users may experience prolonged periods of exaltation when they feel that with no effort they have reached the heights of philosophical profundity. Hitherto complex social and personal problems appear dazzlingly simple. Their awareness of what goes on in themselves and in the world at large becomes marvelously enhanced. But then, as with physiological addictions so with this intellectual one, reality claims its revenge: the real world fails to conform to a drug-induced fantasy. Real problems return and, with them, a feeling of incompleteness and fatigue on the part of the addict. He soon craves another all-explaining formula which would save him from thinking through a problem.

Can the "generation gap" explain all our current discontents? No, we ought to keep in mind that we live in a "post-industrial society." "Alienation" of the young is a world-wide problem. But here in America our particular trouble is that there is no one for our young people to "identify with." (Think how different and fortunate in this respect was the situation of young Americans in the era, say, of Benjamin Harrison or Calvin Coolidge.) We must inspire them with a new sense of purpose, restructure our society, give the young a piece of the action. But wait: are our young gloomily alienated, or do they essentially exemplify and embody the hopeful and regenerating Consciousness Three?

The world of platitudes does not remain stationary. Some wear out and lose favor with the sophisticated public (*e.g.,* how long since we were last urged to "listen to what the radicals were saying since they might tell us something"?); but their place is taken by new ones. Scraps and pieces of what passes for philosophical or sociological wisdom, echoes of something Marx or Freud had said, find a synthesis; this product, then, if successful, becomes a stock-in-trade for panels and commissions, writers of editorials and politicians' speeches. People begin to repeat it; perhaps at first a bit self-consciously and timidly (won't somebody have the bad taste to ask: What does it mean?) but then with increasing confidence and, finally, the conviction that, yes, what Professor Y or Senator X has been saying does in fact express the essence of our problems and the challenge which has been staring us in the face, but which has been ignored until. . . .

Public figures may defy powerful platitudes only at a considerable risk. Perhaps it is less damaging to offend an influential constituency than to wonder aloud whether the generation gap actually exists; whether relevance is the most efficacious remedy for our troubled schools, and what is meant by alienation. Even President Nixon recently felt constrained to bow his head to the generation gap, if one may forgive the mixed metaphor, and in order to refute the accusation of cold indifference to the young, to issue a ringing invitation for a partnership between the idealistic youth and the Establishment?

It will not do to object that this ascendance of platitudes has been of long standing, that slogans, vague maxims, and generalities have always been an important part of our political and intellectual fare. In democratic politics, slogans and sometimes purposely vague general statements have often served as a preamble to or a summary of concrete programs and proposals. But it is in the intellectual sphere that this current surge of vagueness has been most startling and disturbing. When it comes to things of the mind, progress has meant a movement from vagueness to concreteness, relentless questioning of even the most tantalizing abstractions: what *does* it mean? And when it concerns an application of philosophy to human behavior, it has always been accompanied by impatience with high-sounding formulas and the demands for specific proposals and remedies. Our current enslavement by the forces of platitude cannot, thus, be viewed with equanimity. In fact, as I shall try to demonstrate, it poses a greater threat to our educational system and indirectly to our democratic institutions than any so-called extremism.

IT IS STRIKING how much the language of advertisements and the style of public relations have invaded the political and intellectual world. *"Ford has a better idea,"* proclaims the television set, and then in elucidation, *"it is a going thing."* We then shift to a televised program on higher education. The panelists will gravely agree that university courses lack relevance. How is this relevance to be instilled? Well, they need to be focused around the idea of service to the community. Only thus will the vast resources of idealism of our young men and women be tapped, only then will they stop being alienated. Such is the intimidating farce of a fashionable platitude that few in the audience, whether Democrats, Republicans, or anarchists, will have the temerity to admit even to themselves that the whole discussion consisted of stringing together largely meaningless generalities, or explaining one by another, and yet in the end saying nothing which would help anybody to cope with real problems of the real world. It happens to be "the going thing."

But we cannot qualify such exercises as harmless. When it comes to buying a car, most people, whatever propaganda they have been exposed to, will still be capable of assessing their prospective purchase in terms of concrete advantages and disadvantages the given model offers. But in education, as in politics, indoctrination in vague and platitudinous concepts tears at the roots of intellectual discrimination, and hampers (if, indeed, it does not make impossible) a rational choice. Where is the search for relevance going to carry our schools? Few would argue that it would have been advisable for young Einstein to concentrate on learning something which would have been of immediate value to his fellow men rather than exploring higher mathematics, that young Freud should have practiced medicine among Vienna's poor, and not followed his then very esoteric interests in psychiatry, that young Keynes ought to have been doing something practical and not engrossing himself in economic theory. But the very same people who would readily grant the absurdity of such requirements would still enslave our current education to relevance. And insofar as this platitude is clothed with meaning it comes to this. Young men should not follow their natural bent and intellectual skills, or they should feel guilty about being just mathematicians, economists and biologists, or they should sacrifice their selfish intellectual interests on the altar of social concern and activism. Thus an essentially empty concept may yet have consequences which are real and harmful: young persons get diverted from those pursuits which provide meaning and internal balance for their own lives and which in most cases would eventually enrich society as well. At the time when they can learn so much to their own and others' benefit, young men and women are relentlessly propagandized to become addicted to vapid moralizing, and to ineffectual anger and melancholy.

Some would extend this indoctrination beyond the college years into high school, perhaps even into grade school. Here, the fad born out of a platitude reaches proportions of a crime against a whole generation. The period which is really irreplaceable for storing up knowledge and developing skills for the rest of one's life is to be devoted instead to this repetitious chewing over of "issues," of pupils spending their time and energy on subjects which are either useless, or about which enough information can be gathered by a casual look at the daily paper. In the innovative school of this brave new world students would hold forth on ecology and abortion but learn little biology, discuss Communist China's role in the U.N. and the rights and wrongs of Vietnam but fail to master a single foreign language, identify the main areas of injustice in our society but scorn history as irrelevant. The young would arrive—many of them already do, as a matter of fact—at adulthood in a state of mental fatigue, aimless agitation and anger, incapable of that discriminating and purposeful approach to public affairs which democracy calls for in its citizens.

The current ascendance of platitudes threatens not only our own education but, both through it and apart from it, the future of democratic institutions in this country. The process of attrition of democracy begins with the individual citizen's diffidence in his own judgment; his feeling that even concerning subjects hitherto considered susceptible to common sense he must defer to the self-proclaimed expert; his intimidation by rhetoric or a fashionable platitude; his fear that by asking "but what does it mean?" and "how would it work in practice?" he would bare his ignorance, lack of sophistication, or selfishness. The older type of demagogue has been joined by a new one; the former exploited fears of the proverbial ignorant multitude, the latter exploits anxieties, the sense of guilt to a semi-sophisticated audience. The widow of a great Russian poet destroyed by Stalin well delineates the tragedy of the Russian radical intellectuals who were drawn through this process and in the name of the loftiest sounding ideals to submit to the most absolute tyranny. She writes:

> In the pre-revolutionary era there had already been this craving for an all-embracing idea which would explain everything in the world and bring about universal harmony at one go ... This explained the progressive loss of a sense of reality ... The decisive part in the subjugation of intelligentsia was played not by terror (though God knows there was enough of it), but by the word "Revolution" which none of them could bear to give up ... It is a word to which whole nations have succumbed.*

Pragmatism, and a sense of proportion and concreteness, constitute the first line of defense against demagoguery both of the old and the new style. We have an example in recent American history of how a potentially dangerous trend was stemmed not through the invocation of high moral imperatives, but by putting the vague allegations that there were some dark demonic forces at large in society to a concrete test. McCarthyism was an attempt to build upon a few facts a vast structure of conspiracy and treason. The known facts could hardly support this structure, but many people were too distrustful of their own judgment to realize the full absurdity of Senator Joseph McCarthy's rhetoric. There was a justifiable feeling of frustration and anger about the postwar world, about the festering international conflict, about setbacks to democracy and liberal institutions in the face of American exertions and sacrifices. Tales of widespread treason and conspiracy sounded alluring as against the hard task of thinking through the complex reality of international relations. McCarthyism also exploited the moralistic strain in

---

*Nadezhda Mandelstam, *Hope against Hope*, pp. 162, 126.

national thinking. Failures in policy could not be attributed to errors of judgment and the inescapable facts of world politics; they resulted from moral depravity in high places. "Twenty years of treason" was the formula intended to convey the full sense of the immorality of the Establishment under the successive Democratic administrations since 1933 (and at one point the Senator expanded the time span and talked of twenty-*two* years of treason). The rhetoric and the legal power of slander wielded by the Senator were so intimidating, the case for protest and indignation endowed with such superficial validity (China *had* been lost to the Communists, a handful of Communists *had* infiltrated official Washington) that many reasonable people eschewed a direct confrontation with McCarthyism and some pleaded with the Senator to work within the system, *i.e.,* to be more moderate and discriminating in his attacks.

McCarthyism received its mortal wound when the Senator was constrained to plead a concrete case. Through the televised hearings, the country could assess his charge that the promotion of an Army dentist with alleged subversive affiliations indicated the presence of a widespread Communist conspiracy. For all the numerous theatrical and other tragicomic aspects of those hearings, it is fair to say that it was the essential triviality of the proved and provable facts, as against the vast historical forces with which they were allegedly connected, which impressed itself on the nation's consciousness. The spell was broken. The people's minds were freed from the superstitious awe of all those formulas and incantations which explained all our troubles and disappointments so simply and convincingly. Life—and, with it, the problem of Communism—was, alas, more complex.

The case for McCarthyism, as is the case with many current arguments of the New Left, rested on certain unexamined platitudes which derived superficial validity from certain undeniable facts and contrasts between official professions and facts. America was the most powerful state in the world; she was dedicated to freedom and democracy. How come, then, that a few years after the war which this country had fought in the name of those ideals, millions of Poles, Czechs, *et al.,* found themselves under grievous tyranny? The Pacific war had been fought allegedly to save China for the free world. Yet by 1950 China was more firmly under an autocratic, and as it *then* seemed, foreign domination than she had been in 1941. And so today there is the obvious contrast between the professed U.S. aim to bring democracy and peace to Southeast Asia and the grim reality of the Vietnam war; between the vastness of this country's resources and widespread pockets of poverty in this society. Explanations which begin with "there are no easy answers . . .," or the "ineluctable forces of history," are perhaps fine for an academic panel (and even in academic circles moralistic ranting has become fashionable of late). But in times of crisis and anxiety people thirst for simpler answers: treason in high places; the evil designs of the military-industrial complex.

And, in fact, there are simple answers for a great number of problems which have bedeviled this country in its internal and foreign policies. But they are not to be found in the moral depravity or betrayal of those in high or low places, rather for the most part in the failure of intelligence, or (to escape the ambiguity) in the failure of mind, reason, sensible analysis. President Roosevelt's advisers had an insufficient understanding of Stalin's Russia and Chiang Kai-shek's China. President Johnson's counsellors showed a similar insensitivity where it came to the intertwined problems of international Communism in crisis and the civil war in Indochina. The intellectual error was compounded and aggravated in each case by the propensity of the American leaders to represent—and the American public to expect—every American policy to be an exercise in high moral virtue. It would have been found shocking for the president of the United States, or a high government official, to declare that we were fighting alongside the Chinese and the Russians not because their governments shared our devotion to democratic ideals, but simply on account of having an enemy in common; or that we were not fighting for democracy in Southeast Asia but that the interest of this country urged that we should help a friendly but inefficient authoritarian regime against an unfriendly and much more efficient one. Such declarations would have been classified as cynical avowals of power politics, a shameful repudiation of that idealism which ought to be the guiding principle of policies of the United States.

Yet it is precisely this unrealism which has been productive of the most immoral consequences in international politics, those lofty moral platitudes which, when inevitably punctured, bred cynicism and a paralysis of will. Since the first World War did not make the world safe for democracy, the American people became all the more inclined to indulge in self-righteous isolationism, which undoubtedly helped bring about fascist aggression and the Second World War. An absurdly idealized vision of Stalin's Russia, and palpably unrealistic hopes placed on the United Nations were to breed postwar reactions which still haunt us. From a fatuous belief that Soviet policies could be constrained by the principles of the Atlantic Charter, American policies shifted to an opposite extreme and became frozen in a posture of stern anti-Communist virtue. Those opportunities for an accommodation—however temporary and precarious with the USSR, opportunities which undoubtedly existed especially in the 1950s, and which would have saved the world much danger and suffering—were ignored or frittered away, largely through the insistence of Washington that the Communists must prove a change of heart, that they negotiate in good faith before we could bargain with them.

Realism in Southeast Asia should have dictated prudent

cost accounting; prevention of a Communist takeover of South Vietnam could have justified a small American military presence, and a proportionate expenditure. But, again, the moralistic extravagance of American thinking about foreign policy triggered off an overcommitment which has largely destroyed the country we sought to save for the "free world;" and it led to as yet incalculable deplorable consequences at home and elsewhere in the world. Vietnam brought to a sizeable and influential segment of American public opinion the by-now predictable reaction: since American policies were unsucessful, they reflected the inherent wickedness of their makers, and in fact of American society at large. It has not been cynicism but an uncritical acceptance of certain moralistic platitudes which inspired the disastrous policies of the last decade in Vietnam. It has not been a realistic exposure of those policies but moralistic platitudes of another, masochistic variety, which have inspired opposition to them. Those analysts and politicians who have tried to inject a rational element into the discussion found themselves assailed from both sides. Did they propose to deliver South Vietnam to Communist tyranny (as if the amount of destruction and suffering inflicted upon the unhappy country had not already surpassed the potential of oppression by the most tyrannical regime)? Were they denying the national-liberation character of the struggle (as if the success of the Viet Cong did not reflect their superior organization and ruthlessness)? For the extremes on both sides the real struggle had long ago ceased to be in Indo-China. It is here in the United States that, as they see each other, the capitalist and imperialist Establishment is grappling with treason and anti-Americanism.

It is often asserted that the war has divided American society. But this is imprecise. What has divided American society has been the moral rhetoric, always and excessively present in American politics, which has been vastly enhanced by the unsuccessful and, to most people, incomprehensible war. It is bad enough when this moral rhetoric accompanies a virtual national consensus. For it then produces the eventually damaging oversimplifications: *e.g.*, democracies struggling against the absolute evil of totalitarianism in World War II; or the free world standing up against "Godless Communism" in the postwar era. But what we have now in this country is not so much divided judgment but unified moral indignation venting itself against different targets, a clash of moral imperatives—in brief, a situation in which it is difficult for reason to prevail, for this country to extricate itself from a difficult situation in Asia without a legacy of feelings of betrayal and rage on the part of a sizeable element in American society.

To an important extent our failures in foreign policy have, then, reflected the failure of American education to present a realistic picture of the world, to teach *not* that the moral element in international politics is unimportant but precisely that to establish a more moral international order we must have a realistic view of the over-all situation. The genius of democratic politics has consisted (at least until fairly recently) in the ability of various groups and interests in society to engage in day-to-day conflicts and tests of strength without moralistic passion, in devising pragmatic techniques for problem-solving without asking the often unanswerable question, What are moral rights and wrongs in each case? No labor dispute could ever be settled if the contestants would defer the issue of dollars and cents, until the great question of respective rights of Labor and Capital were first decided, until the problems of moral guilt and psychic sufferings of the respective parties had first to be ascertained. Were we to ask, as indeed has become increasingly the fashion, who are the Guilty and who are the Righteous in the case of every area of conflict and dispute in our society, our political life would resolve itself into a series of cataclysmic battles with

anarchy and then authoritarianism the eventual and inevitable outcome. Liberalism in politics—the liberal outlook
in politics—has been made possible through precisely the
same process which has made possible the advance of science
and learning: search for concreteness, the once (and, evidently, now again) iconoclastic belief that all varieties of
progress are best served, not through seeking perfection or
the ultimate truth, but through an increased mastery of
intellectual skills and techniques. "What is life?" is indeed a
fundamental question, but where would we be if the study of
concrete properties of matter, of the nature of the living cell,
had had to await a consensus of philosophers and divines on
that admittedly intriguing problem? And so, as far as
political institutions are concerned, democracy has fared
badly where the belief in self-evident and inalienable rights
has been allowed to preclude the search for practical institutions and procedures to enable the government to function.

Totalitarian ideologies do not, on the other hand, allow
such separation between matters of faith and of politics. The
citizen of Soviet Russia and of Communist China not only
lives under a specific political and social system, he is
required at least outwardly to accept it as a matter of faith.
And that faith exacts not only, as in the case of real religions,
a specific moral code, but also a whole set of specific beliefs
concerning the arts, sciences, etc. Communism requires both
the arts and sciences to conform to certain canons as well as
to be relevant, *i.e.,* to stress themes thought desirable by the
leader or the ruling elite. Not only is the individual forced to
do what the state wants him to, but insofar as it can, a
totalitarian regime tries to suppress what might be called his
inner pluralism, to leave no sphere of belief, education, or
amusement free from its dictation. And the doctrine, no
matter how rationally conceived, becomes in the hands of the
totalitarian state a dogma. One ends up with a truly preposterous situation where one nation of several hundred

million people worships a man in his late seventies as the supreme authority on all human pursuits from philosophy to swimming, where in another a group of middle-aged bureaucrats presumes to dictate what lines of research, what themes are allowable and relevant in biology or in poetry and fiction. This enslavement of the mind has been made possible not only because of the monopoly of power wielded by the state but, even more basically, because of two major beliefs totalitarian education has instilled in the minds of its victims: *1)* that there are some ineluctable historical laws which ordain the present (in many cases, admittedly unhappy) situation in which millions of Russians and Chinese find themselves, and *2)* that there can be men who are infallible experts on the relationship of morals and politics, and that to challenge the edicts of Mao or the Politburo on those subjects or even to ask what concrete meaning lies behind those vague formulas (proletarian solidarity, building socialism, etc.) in the name of which they justify their power and privilege, is at best to exhibit immoral selfishness, and at worst to become an enemy of the people. It is not so much physical fear which keeps hundreds of millions enslaved, as it is their diffidence induced by a combination of indoctrination and apathy. Hence the inability to apply criteria of common sense to the alleged historical laws and moral imperatives as proclaimed by the totalitarian regime; hence the inability to see through hollow platitudes designed to rationalize whole nations into surrendering their judgment to a few.

WHAT DOES THIS have to do with America's schools and universities and American society? Well, while there has been here no authoritarian state trying to enforce a uniformity of thought, there has been an *un*concerted effort from the most diverse sources to change the American thinking on society from its traditionally secular and pragmatic pattern to an essentially religious one. Many of our current social critics and philosophers, whether in or outside academic life, are not so much theorists trying to work out a coherent structure of social action, or reformers addressing themselves to specific problems, as they are would-be prophets uttering vague threats and incantations, and pronouncing curses and damnations on post-industrial society unless, in a manner not specified, it is reborn to conform to Dr. *X's* vague notions of what constitutes mental health or Professor *Y's* participatory democracy. Behind them there has grown (and, in the last decade, by leaps and bounds) a veritable new class, half a priesthood and half a bureaucracy, which has made repetition of those vague generalities and incantations the basis of its claim for support by governments, schools, and foundations.

Milovan Djilas broke many years ago with the Yugoslav Communist regime of which he was one of the highest officials. He went then through a process of ideological decompression which led him from a belief in a more democratic form of Communism to a resolute rejection of most of the doctrinal elements of Marxism. At a fairly early point in his evolution he saw clearly how Communism bred this New Class with its vested interest in indoctrinating the people in murky ideological and moralistic slogans, and in confusing and concealing the real problems and alternatives in economics and politics. What Djilas, in the bitterness of his disillusionment, failed to allow for was the fact that many members of the New Class (as he himself had been some years before) are genuinely convinced that they are conferring a boon on society, that their constant interference with and censoriousness in regard to the individual citizen's life is amply justified by wider social needs. And yet the day-to-day oppressiveness of living in a totalitarian society is due not only to a leader or leaders pronouncing those infallible dicta on politics and life in general, but to the whole horde of officials, professors, and journalists who because they are public servants, *i.e.,* on the government payroll, assume that they have the duty of admonishing, warning, and exhorting their fellow citizens, chastising their private and selfish concerns, demanding that they in fact sacrifice their individuality on the altar of public interest. Has not something of the kind been happening in America? Have not our universities been breeding this new class—sociologists and newspapermen and administrators who, over and above their expertise, feel it their right and obligation to tell the mass of citizens what they must do, and what kind of social behavior is or is not moral?

Democracy was made possible in the first place by people liberating themselves from vague fears and guilt feelings, and by seeking concrete answers to concrete social and political problems. And that, in turn, implied rejecting claims of any class or priesthood that its expertise in things moral and spiritual entitled it to lay down laws in politics and economics. But today, in an age of dazzling advances in science and when organized religions have grown confused and apologetic about their traditional and legitimate authority, we appear to be witnessing a rebirth of an essentially medieval approach to problems of society and politics.

Many of the most prevalent clichés and slogans have a clearly religious symbolism. When an institution, be it a university or a corporation, is called upon to acknowledge that it is elitist, or racist, or sexist, or what-have-you, it is obviously called upon to confess that it is in a state of sin, and only after such an admission can penance begin. To a nineteenth-century liberal (or, for that matter, Karl Marx) it would have appeared the height of absurdity to postulate that an *institution* can have moral attributes. He would have found equally incomprehensible—a relic from the tribal past—the attribution of specific moral qualities to specific age-groups. What is the ability to communicate with the young, to bridge that famous gap, but something mysterious, akin to the quality of religious grace? The urge which drives some young people into communes, and away from the treadmill of materialistic and competitive society, is recognizably identical to that which drove them in the Middle Ages to monasteries and eremitical existence. Several ancient heresies were accused, in the wake of their extirpation by the forces of orthodoxy of preaching the damnable doctrine that since the world of the senses was evil in any case, all forms of sexual license and aberration were allowable until the state of absolute perfection was reached. Here, again, there are tantalizing parallels with our own day. With all due respect to those who have coined the term, our allegedly post-industrial society exhibits an amazing number of characteristics of a very, very pre-industrial one.

The heavily religious undertone of much of what passes for sophisticated social discourse today explains much of its vagueness. One looks in vain in the works of our leading social critics for a concrete program or blueprint. Many of them are interested in expatiating lengthily and repetitiously on evil, our competitive and materialistic society, and salvation, in the light of some very hazy utopia of universal participation and harmony. There is a ready identification of the damned—or, at least, the corrupt (the Establishment, the middle-aged middle class)—and those pure in spirit, the young and (though, nowadays, rather rarely) the working class, or the proletariat, as those with an incurable nostalgia for Marxism still call it. But will a man who sees inequality as the root cause of evil propose a specific upper limit on personal income? Not likely. Such details are thought to be out of place in a philosophical disquisition on alienation; and, for some very obvious reasons, they would not be popular with some of the most strenuous bewailers of the false values of our society. There has been a considerable body of criticism, much of it justified, of the performance and influence of the great business corporation. But will the critics of corporate power propose what used to be a classical recipe for curbing big business and subjecting it to the public weal, *i.e.,* nationalization? Plainly, no. For most Americans, a plea for nationalization of big business, and thus for disposing of at least one half of the military-industrial complex, would evoke a vision of U.S. Steel or General Motors being run on the same pattern, and perhaps with the same efficiency, as the U.S. Post Office.

Much of the discussion of other social problems and grievances is veiled in the same "whatever-we-might-do-about-it-we-must-feel-guilty" attitude. Among those agitated about the racial problems in this country, there are undoubtedly persons whose main concern is the most expeditious removal of the remaining forms of discrimination; but for others this is a very pleasing demonstration of the inherent wickedness of society, a hair-shirt not to be discarded whatever the improvement. It is easy to detect a similar syndrome in relation to poverty, pollution, and other outstanding social ailments. Suggestions that these are problems susceptible of solution short of a cataclysmic or utopian transformation of our whole society, *i.e.,* they are mechanical failures rather than evidence of deep moral depravity, are met with distaste if not indeed indignation. Such has been the saturation of the current social and intellectual scene with gloomy moralism that even pornography has of late been considered a form of social criticism, rather than a diversion.

Such opinions may appear extravagant, and it would be an exaggeration to assert that a great majority of Americans are engaged in such gloomy introspection or have become converts to this peculiar brand of social masochism. But certainly this mood, parading as a philosophy, has been widely propagated among what might be called, for lack of a better term, the educated class in this country. A cursory glance at the national press and at our leading magazines will confirm how widespread this mood is. It has permeated television and the whole amusement industry. It has even made inroads in what once seemed the impregnable bastion of the carefree non-cerebral attitude toward life, American sports. A long-haired or bearded athlete, bewailing how irrelevant are his pursuits to problems of alienation, bemoaning his (highly paid) servitude to the capitalist bosses, has become perhaps the most distinctive epitome of today's America. The ritual of politics, once so full of both conscious and unconscious humor, has now been permeated with this catastrophism. A politician, striving for an office, will still (but only in front of an unsophisticated audience) crack jokes and discourse in a lighter vein. But his mood will change if he addresses a college or middle-class audience, or if he tries to impart to the national press and other media that he is a man for our troubled times and not a throwback to the scandalously complacent '50s or unabashedly corny '40s. His mood would then be one of measured anguish, of frank avowal of various and vast areas of iniquity in American life. He would couple this frankness with a plea to the young not to give up, to work within the system, for with reordered priorities this country might still be saved and might even be worth saving. A shrewd politician will try to improve his image by hobnobbing with more moderate advocates of dissent among the social scientists. He will finally venture into the lions' den by appearing at one of the leading (*i.e.,* both in terms of its reputation and its student turbulence, the two being almost synonymous) universities. Here, if he is lucky, he will be received with just the right amount of abuse from the extremists and just the right kind of thoughtful attention from would-be workers within the system. But it is not the young that an aspiring politician is really wooing through such hazardous ventures. It is their parents who are to be impressed. Here is a man who can communicate, who can deflect their progeny's wrath and perhaps channel their savage energies into some positive action. So, if elected, he might bring an end to alienation and to those other mysterious ailments and afflictions which the experts have detected and which, though they are beyond a layman's comprehension, are evidently real and threatening.

THE TOTAL PICTURE adds up to what an English writer claimed life is in general—comedy for those who think, tragedy for those who feel. It is in a way inexpressibly funny, something which calls for the pen of a great writer: it is the spectacle of a whole society experiencing a sort of cosmic hangover. Politicians and clerics and professors are lost in gloomy ruminations. Aspiring young scholars, in a frantic search for relevance and notice, explore the past for yet another example of historical villainy by the United States, search out the present for as yet neglected areas of oppression and social injustice, and peer into the future for some additional form of catastrophe which will afflict this madly materialistic and competitive society even if it should be spared by the bomb, pollution, and urban violence.

There is, in fact, some heartening evidence of a budding counter-revolution of common-sense. Neither society as a whole nor its younger component has lost entirely that sense of humor and proportion which has been one of the strongest influences in the achievement and maintaining of the American democratic process. But the present situation is still disturbing because that counter-revolution may come too late; or it may be superseded by a period of obscurantism of a right-wing variety in reaction to the current one of left-wing and ritualistic liberalism. True liberalism—one which seeks concrete solutions for concrete problems, one which employs a rational analysis rather than apocalyptic visions of damnation and salvation—may thus become a waning force in American life, and its disappearance could not but be followed by that of democratic institutions.

One may recall what some previous excesses in moralistic self-indulgence have done to American society. The example of Prohibition and the damage done through it to law-abiding habits of a whole generation does not require elaboration. It is not so much any specific policies but those pretensions of national moral superiority which underlay isolationism that were so harmful and contributed to the train of events which concluded in World War II.

The fact is that the present thrust and content of moralistic self-indulgence has been neatly reversed from the 1920s; many Americans now find tantalizing the contemplation of national wickedness, just as then the country congratulated itself on its superior virtue. This may please a believer in the irony of history, but does not make the phenomenon any less dangerous. The need for a rational approach to politics, detached though not independent of the moral questions involved, is greater than ever before. Insofar as international politics is concerned, one does not have to spell out the reasons. "Let justice be done even if the whole world perish" is an ethical maxim which the progress of technology has made too literally feasible to serve us as a guide-line in politics. Yet if one observes the current debate on foreign policy it is striking how much it is pervaded by this maxim and how much proponents of clashing viewpoints, whether on Vietnam, the Near East, or Africa, appear to be confident of what justice is and what it requires us to do regardless of the risks involved. In domestic politics one hears repeatedly what seem like echoes of a device of the nineteenth-century Russian radical: "All that can be destroyed must be destroyed." Here, again, the implications of such exuberance are quite different from what they were even for the most thoroughgoing nineteenth-century anarchist.

THE PRESENT SITUATION makes the general public as well as the proverbial sober politician accept as part of the general political discourse those ideas and activities which in fact represent forms of quasi-religious obsession or, in very extreme forms on both ends of the political spectrum, of mass mental derangement. Such movements do not have political postulates; in fact, it is difficult to accuse them of seeking political power. Their aim is to strike down the ungodly, be they alleged Communists in high places and in education, or the capitalist bosses and American imperialists. The state—American society— is a collective Anti-Christ to be fought and thwarted. It is, accordingly, instructive to consider those foreign states and societies which have attracted the greatest sympathy of the more extreme branches of our New Left. Theoretically, one might suppose that those desirous of a basic socialist transformation of our society would be interested and sympathetic to Yugoslavia. Here is a Communist country which has managed to preserve a degree of independence from the two super-powers, and where you have a socialist economy and one-party rule but also a greater amount of intellectual and social freedom than anywhere else in the Communist world. And, as such, Yugoslavia has enjoyed excellent relations with the most radical governments in the Third World. Yet to our extreme (and perhaps also to the not-so-extreme) New Left in America, Yugoslavia is of no interest and for obvious reasons. She has had fairly friendly relations with the United States. The same factor accounts for the complete disinterest in those circles in Rumania, another impeccably Communist country which has sought to pursue its own path independent of the main power blocs. The Soviet Union, once the magnet of radical dissent in this country, now fails to excite native anti-Americanism. In contrast, it is Communist China, Cuba, and North Vietnam (in that order, for what is North Vietnam doing *negotiating* with the United States?) which appeal to our romantic extremists. It is interesting to speculate whether their loyalty will long survive initiation of diplomatic ties between Peking and the United States, a dramatic improvement of relations with Castro, and peace in Vietnam. One suspects not.

The widespread misconception of what extremism represents is a result of that erosion of the rational approach to politics which has been such a characteristic phenomenon of the last decade. It would be possible, though this is not the place, to observe parallel phenomena in other spheres of national life: in the decline of the arts where the search for relevance has often had results as preposterous as those in education; in the field of morals where American puritanism turned in upon itself, leading to that joyless and frantic licentiousness which is extolled as a blow at ancient hypocrisies, but which is in fact as much a rejection of intelligent hedonism as is asceticism.

In writing about those varied though interconnected phenomena, there is a great temptation to do precisely what has been decried here, to postulate one or several cosmic causes, or to indulge in a kind of demonology, identifying individuals or a class who, through their malevolence or in pursuit of some plot, have brought this society to a condition which is as ridiculous as it is lamentable, and dangerous to itself and to the world. But, as it has been argued here, there are no major cosmic causes, only a great variety of errors and of failures to apply common sense to problems which call for it, rather than for the alleged wisdom of a self-proclaimed expert. There are no major villains or plotters, but a lot of people in influential positions, whether in politics, education or journalism, who lack the intellectual self-confidence to defy fashionable platitudes. And exploiting their diffidence and that of the educated public at large, there has grown a whole class of producers and propagators of those platitudes. It is those people who, often with conviction and a sense of rendering public service, grind out in their books, columns, lectures, and sermons this debilitating concoction which has come to pass for sophistication and humanitarianism in matters concerning society and politics.

FROM WHERE can improvement come? One is thrown back upon one's faith in democracy's capacity to grow tired and to see through moralistic fads and quasi-religious cults posing as ideologies or scientific theories of society.

If there is to be such a counter-revolution of common sense, then part of it will have to be a reassessment of the role, potentialities, and limitations of education. For education within the last two decades has become what business had been in the U.S. of the 1920s, an object of worship and the repository of excessive hopes for the improvement of society. As with business, then so with education, it has recently been assumed that here at hand is the master agent in social and individual change and improvement, not only in those areas which are within its province, but also in those of morals, politics, and religion. A corollary of the worship of business was a belief that from unlimited economic expansion and private enterprise would come solutions for all social and political ailments; that within the business community were to be found the guiding maxims of wisdom on domestic and international politics. Though the analogy should not be carried too far, hasn't something similar been allowed to take place in regard to education? What is only one (though a supremely important) area of national life and of individual experience has become confused with life as a whole. Nothing is more pathetic in this respect than the often-voiced complaint—another example of a journalistic slogan which has become a sociological platitude—that our schools do not educate "the whole man." As if they did not have enough trouble teaching English, arithmetic, and imparting the rudiments of civilized behavior.

For the American university the beginning of wisdom and reform must lie in acknowledging that there are clear limits to what education can do for the individual and society, and that it has been the attempt to transgress those limits which has been responsible for most of our troubles with education. We must grant the merchants of platitudes that they are right when they hold student disorders to be but a symptom of a much deeper disorder affecting our educational institutions. But we disagree with them when it comes to the diagnosis of that disorder. The American university ought to be returned to its proper purposes: promoting learning and advancing knowledge. As such, it will become again a source of strength to society and of lasting satisfaction to its students. It will produce studies of social and political problems designed for intellectual illumination rather than the procurement for their authors of positions in Washington, or the affection of fashionable radicals, or both. It will train public servants, in the true sense of the words, rather than busybodies and careerists imbued with the belief that their superior intellect entitles them to lay down laws to the ignorant multitude and the vulgar politician. It will continue to shelter dissent, *i.e.,* radicalism, even of the most extreme kind, but not obsession masquerading as such. Those benefits to society will flow from those conferred upon its students. A real university instills in its students (well, in a great majority of them anyway) not only intellectual skills, but intellectual curiosity which is the best antidote to that boredom and despair incorrectly called alienation.

From our current perspective such expectations may well appear extravagant, perhaps even utopian. But it is in the pursuit of such a utopia—and how infuriating to think that it was within sight not so many years ago—that the American university will become once more a civilized and civilizing institution.

ABOUT THE AUTHOR

ADAM ULAM is one of America's most distinguished scholars in the field of politics and history. He is a Professor of Government at Harvard University and a Fellow of the Russian Research Center there. He was born in Poland in 1922, attended Brown University (1943), and received his Ph.D. from Harvard in 1947. His first book was a study of the *Philosophical Foundations of English Socialism* (1951), and his most recent is a history, published by Viking Press, of America and Russia since World War II, entitled *The Rivals.* His famous book on *Lenin and the Bolsheviks* (1966) has been translated into German, Spanish, Italian and French. Professor Ulam lives in Cambridge, Massachusetts with his wife and two sons.